P9-DVE-504

DATE DUE

FE 8 88			
MY 13 '94			
MY 27 '94			
DE 9 '94			
DE 27 '95			

Boswell's Life of
Johnson

Modern Critical Interpretations

James Boswell's
Life of Samuel Johnson

Modern Critical Interpretations

These and other titles in preparation

James Boswell's
Life of Samuel Johnson

Edited and with an introduction by
Harold Bloom
Sterling Professor of the Humanities
Yale University

Chelsea House Publishers ◊ *1986*

NEW YORK ◊ NEW HAVEN ◊ PHILADELPHIA

Copyright © 1986 by Chelsea House Publishers, a
division of Chelsea House Educational
Communications, Inc.
  345 Whitney Avenue, New Haven, CT 06511
  133 Christopher Street, New York, NY 10014
  5014 West Chester Pike, Edgemont, PA 19028

Introduction copyright © 1986 by Harold Bloom

∞   The paper used in this publication meets the
minimum requirements of the American National
Standard for Permanence of Paper for Printed Library
Materials Z39.48–1984

Printed and bound in the United States of America

Library of Congress Cataloging-in-Publication Data
Main entry under title:

Boswell's Life of Johnson.

    (Modern critical interpretations)
    Bibliography: p.
    Includes index.
    Contents: Literary form in factual narrative/
Ralph Rader—Boswell's control of aesthetic distance/
Paul Alkon—The life of Johnson/Frederick A.
Pottle—[etc.]
    1. Boswell, James, 1740–1795. Life of Samuel
Johnson—Addresses, essays, lectures. 2. Biography
(as a literary form)—Addresses, essays, lectures.
3. Authors, English—18th century—Biography—
Addresses, essays, lectures. I. Bloom, Harold. II. Series.

PR3533.B63B669   1986   828'.609 [B]   85-26974
ISBN 0-87754-946-X

Contents

Editor's Note

This volume gathers together essays that are, in its editor's judgment, capable studies of the greatest literary biography in the English language. The editor is grateful to Ms. Marena Fisher for her dedicated labor in helping to locate, and evaluate, several of these essays, which are reprinted here in the chronological order of their original publication.

The book begins with the editor's introduction, which contrasts Boswell's self-consciousness as both biographer and subject in the *Tour to the Hebrides* and the *Life of Johnson*. Ralph Rader's shrewd analysis of "literary form in factual narrative," as manifested in the *Life*, emphasizes how problematic the relation is between factual literature and what we want to call "truth." Boswell's remarkable control of aesthetic distance is demonstrated, and praised, by Paul Alkon, who regards the occasional falterings in this control as being no more than qualifications of Boswell's grand achievement.

Frederick A. Pottle, Boswell's supreme scholar-critic, brilliantly and economically states the crucial achievement of Boswell in the *Life*: to render conversations with Johnson as though they were pure Johnson, and yet to make them "the quintessence of Boswell's view of Johnson." In contrast, Richard Schwartz gives us "Johnson's Johnson" through the images that Boswell presents of him in the *Life*. Related to that powerful control of images is Boswell's immense tact in deciding what facts to omit in crucial passages of the *Life*, a tact whose aesthetic implications are the subject of William Siebenschuh's keen meditation upon "factual appearance and fictional effects."

Frank Brady's definitive survey of five central issues concerning the *Life* illuminates each of those issues with enormous authority and extraordinary Boswellian learning. This volume ends with a stimulating and experimental study by Patricia Meyer Spacks, whose remarkable book, *Gossip*, is quarried here for a final vision of Boswell's mastery of the difficult relation between "moral and physical truth" in literary biography.

Introduction

I

Boswell's *Life of Johnson* begins with a dedicatory letter to Sir Joshua Reynolds, which includes a paragraph of acutely defensive self-consciousness remarkable even for Boswell:

> In one respect, this Work will, in some passages, be different from the former. In my *Tour*, I was almost unboundedly open in my communications; and from my eagerness to display the wonderful fertility and readiness of Johnson's wit, freely shewed to the world its dexterity, even when I was myself the object of it. I trusted that I should be liberally understood, as knowing very well what I was about, and by no means as simply unconscious of the pointed effects of the satire. I own, indeed, that I was arrogant enough to suppose that the tenour of the rest of the book would sufficiently guard me against such a strange imputation. But it seems I judged too well of the world; for, though I could scarcely believe it, I have been undoubtedly informed, that many persons, especially in distant quarters, not penetrating enough into Johnson's character, so as to understand his mode of treating his friends, have arraigned my judgement, instead of seeing that I was sensible of all that they could observe.

Doubtless, Boswell remembered too well certain attacks upon his *Tour to the Hebrides with Samuel Johnson.* Mrs. Hester Lynch Piozzi, formerly Mrs. Henry Thrale, had accused Boswell of misrepresenting her judgments, while Sir John Hawkins had allowed only a single reference to Boswell in his authorized biography of Johnson, which like Mrs. Piozzi's *Anecdotes of Johnson,* appeared in 1786, five years before Boswell's *Life.* Hawkins disposed of Boswell in one suave sentence: "He had long been solicited by Mr. James Boswell, a native of Scotland, and one that highly valued him, to accompany him in a journey to the Hebrides."

Determined to provoke no more such slights, Boswell disarmingly concludes his dedication to Reynolds with two remarkable sentences: "I have, therefore, in this Work been more reserved; and though I tell nothing but the truth, I have still kept in my mind that the whole truth is not always to be exposed. This, however, I have managed so as to occasion no diminution of the pleasure which my book should afford; though malignity may sometimes be disappointed of its gratifications."

Let us test the "whole truth" in the *Tour* with the "nothing but the truth" of the *Life.* First, from the *Tour:*

> It grew dusky; and we had a very tedious ride for what was called five miles; but I am sure would measure ten. We had no conversation. I was riding forward to the inn at Glenelg, on the shore opposite to Sky, that I might take proper measures, before Dr. Johnson, who was now advancing in dreary silence, Hay leading his horse, should arrive. Vass also walked by the side of his horse, and Joseph followed behind: as therefore he was thus attended, and seemed to be in deep meditation, I thought there could be no harm in leaving him for a little while. He called me back with a tremendous shout, and was really in a passion with me for leaving him. I told him my intentions, but he was not satisfied, and said, 'Do you know, I should as soon have thought of picking a pocket, as doing so.'—*Boswell.* 'I am diverted with you, sir.'—*Johnson.* 'Sir, I could never be diverted with incivility. Doing such a thing, makes one lose confidence in him who has done it, as one cannot tell what he may do next.'—His extraordinary warmth confounded me so much, that I justified myself but lamely to him; yet my intentions were not improper. I wished to get on, to see how we were to be lodged, and how we were to get a boat; all which I thought I could best settle myself, without his having any trouble. To apply his great mind

to minute particulars, is wrong: it is like taking an immense balance, such as is kept on quays for weighing cargoes of ships,—to weigh a guinea. I knew I had neat little scales, which would do better; and that his attention to every thing which falls in his way, and his uncommon desire to be always in the right, would make him weigh, if he knew of the particulars: it was right therefore for me to weigh them, and let him have them only in effect. I however continued to ride by him, finding he wished I should do so.

To spare Johnson the "minute particulars" of lodging and travel, poor Boswell has stumbled into the fundamental error of exposing the great critic to the madness of solitude, peculiarly unendurable in the wastelands of Scotland, yet always terribly hard upon the sociable Johnson, with his precarious balance. Yet this seems a mild provocation when contrasted with a characteristic moment in the *Life*:

When we were alone, I introduced the subject of death, and endeavoured to maintain that the fear of it might be got over. I told him that David Hume said to me, he was no more uneasy to think he should *not be* after this life, than that he *had not been* before he began to exist. JOHNSON. 'Sir, if he really thinks so, his perceptions are disturbed; he is mad: if he does not think so, he lies. He may tell you, he holds his finger in the flame of a candle, without feeling pain; would you believe him? When he dies, he at least gives up all he has.' BOSWELL. 'Foote, Sir told me, that when he was very ill he was not afraid to die.' JOHNSON. 'It is not true, Sir. Hold a pistol to Foote's breast, or to Hume's breast, and threaten to kill them, and you'll see how they behave.' BOSWELL. 'But may we not fortify our minds for the approach of death?' Here I am sensible I was in the wrong, to bring before his view what he ever looked upon with horrour; for although when in a celestial frame, in his 'Vanity of human Wishes', he has supposed death to be 'kind Nature's signal for retreat,' from this state of being to 'a happier seat,' his thoughts upon this aweful change were in general full of dismal apprehensions. His mind resembled the vast amphitheatre, the Colisaeum at Rome. In the centre stood his judgement, which, like a mighty gladiator, combated those apprehensions that, like the wild beasts of the *Arena,* were all around in cells, ready to be let out upon him. After

> a conflict, he drove them back into their dens; but not killing them, they were still assailing him. To my question, whether we might not fortify our minds for the approach of death, he answered, in a passion, 'No, Sir, let it alone. It matters not how a man dies, but how he lives. The act of dying is not of importance, it lasts so short a time.' He added, (with an earnest look,) 'A man knows it must be so, and submits. It will do him no good to whine.'
>
> I attempted to continue the conversation. He was so provoked, that he said, 'Give us no more of this;' and was thrown into such a state of agitation, that he expressed himself in a way that alarmed and distressed me; shewed an impatience that I should leave him, and when I was going away, called to me sternly, 'Don't let us meet to-morrow.'

Johnson, a brave man, feared neither death nor dying, yet dreaded judgment, dreaded being damned for having failed to develop all his gifts. Comparison of the two episodes perhaps reveals more circumstantial detail in the *Tour* than in the *Life*, but this is the "whole truth" only in an uninteresting sense. The "nothing but the truth" in the episode from the *Life* may conceal Boswell's experimental meddling with his friend's fears. Boswell, as outrageous a literary figure as Norman Mailer, certainly was capable of goading Johnson deliberately, in order to garner fresh material. In one peculiar moment, Boswell infuriates Johnson by formulating the phantasmagoria of the great man locked up in the Tower, by his enemies, in the company of a newborn babe. Would the Doctor nurture the infant? Would he educate him? Johnson rightly is exasperated, but we, the readers, are rightly charmed. Boswell, on one level, really does want Johnson to play the part of Johnson all the time, almost as though Johnson were the Falstaff of reality.

II

Boswell's "Johnson" is of course, a fiction, but so is Boswell's "Boswell" in the *London Journal*, and so, in a related sense, is Johnson's "Johnson," the Ecclesiastes-like wisdom writer of *The Rambler, Rasselas, The Vanity of Human Wishes*, the *Preface to Shakespeare*, and the *Lives of the Poets*. When we read the *Life of Johnson*, we begin with the assumption that Dr. Samuel Johnson is not of the company of Sir John Falstaff, even though we delight to imagine them both as monarchs of conversation enthroned in their proper context, the tavern. Yet there is a sense in which Johnson is not only a conversational genius in himself, but the cause of grand conversation in other men and women just as Falstaff is the cause of wit in others. Witness Boswell's delicious account of the meeting between Johnson and an old college acquaintance, Edwards, after a separation of some forty-nine years. Nothing could be more memorable than a famous observation by the amiable Edwards: "You are a philosopher, Dr. Johnson. I have tried too in my time to be a philosopher; but, I don't know how, cheerfulness was always breaking in!"

Whether this truly was Edwards's, or is Boswell's own superb invention, we cannot know. What we do know is that Johnson was his own invention, and not Boswell's. Johnson without Boswell has rather a smaller audience now than Boswell without Johnson, but it is fit audience though few. "Boswell with Johnson" might be a proper description for the authorship of the *Life of Johnson*. It may even be divided thus; if *ethos* is the *daimon,* or character is fate, then Johnson is the author of the deepest portion of the *Life*, because Johnson's character is anything but Boswell's creation. The *ethos* of the greatest English writer of wisdom literature is as clearly recognizable in the *Life of Johnson* as it is in the *Life of Savage* or the *Life of Pope*. But if *pathos* is the swerve away from overdetermination, or personality is freedom, then the personality of Johnson, in the *Life of Johnson*, truly is Boswell's creation. So endearing is that personality, so vital is it to us as readers, that Boswell's Johnson, like Shakespeare's Falstaff, has become a permanent image of human freedom. Freedom from what, in Johnson's case? Falstaff is free of the superego, while Johnson is tormented by that psychic agency. Johnson, I think, has so strong an ego that paradoxically he is free of the ego, free of the ego's narcissistic investment in a self, which becomes its own self. Johnson, particularly in Boswell, though uncannily dark, and shadowed by presentiments, does not manifest either of Kierkegaard's two inevitable despairs: the despair of having failed to become oneself, or the still greater despair of having become oneself. It may be Boswell's greatest triumph that he gives us Dr. Johnson as a hero of consciousness, a man strong enough to live without illusions and without deceit.

Boswell's Johnson is eminently a humorist, and though a moralist, he is generally too wise to present his wisdom without humor. There are hundreds of instances in the *Life*, but I have a special fondness for a breakfast conversation between Johnson and Boswell on June 5, 1781, when the doctor was already seventy-two years in age:

> On Tuesday, June 5, Johnson was to return to London. He was very pleasant at breakfast; I mentioned a friend of mine having resolved never to marry a pretty woman. JOHNSON. 'Sir, it is a very foolish resolution to resolve never to marry a pretty woman.

Beauty is of itself very estimable. No, Sir, I would prefer a pretty woman, unless there are objections to her. A pretty woman may be foolish; a pretty woman may be wicked; a pretty woman may not like me. But there is no such danger in marrying a pretty woman as is apprehended; she will not be persecuted if she does not invite persecution. A pretty woman, if she has a mind to be wicked, can find a readier way than another; and that is all.'

"And that is all," but as always with Boswell's Johnson, that is a great deal.

III

Boswell's greatest achievement, in the *Life*, is that he persuades us that his Johnson is *the* Johnson, which many incessant readers of Johnson (myself included) do not like to admit. Yet so strong is Boswell's imagination of Johnson that we tend to read it into Johnson whenever we read the sage, so that we never can be free of Boswell, once we have read the *Life of Johnson*. Even the greatest of modern scholar-critics of Johnson, my teacher W. K. Wimsatt, Jr., who was certainly the most Johnsonian personality I will ever know, is pervaded by Boswell, consciously and unconsciously, throughout his magnificient *The Prose Style of Johnson*. Wimsatt powerfully conveys Johnson's dislike of mere history and related love of biography, which is based upon a dislike of the plainness of fact, not as opposed to fiction, but as opposed to elaboration and its possibilities. On this account, Boswell in the *Life of Johnson* is more Johnsonian than even Johnson could have been. The true test for Boswell's masterpiece would thus be set by Johnson himself, in *Rambler* No. 3:

The task of an author is, either to teach what is not known, or to recommend known truths by his manner of adorning them; either to let new light in upon the mind, and open new scenes to the prospect, or to vary the dress and situation of common objects, so as to give them fresh grace and more powerful attractions, to spread such flowers over the regions through which the intellect has already made its progress, as may tempt it to return, and take a second view of things hastily passed over or negligently regarded.

This task of elaboration by adornment, variation, refinement is the project of both Pope in his poetry and Boswell in the *Life of Johnson*. What Johnson praised in Pope, we must praise in Boswell: if Boswell be not a biographer, where is biography to be found? Boswell is both neoclassical, as suits a follower of Johnson, and an apostle of sentiment, of sensibility and the Sublime, as was inevitable for a literary consciousness in Boswell's own generation. Johnson, though far shrewder and more humane in *praxis* than in critical theory, was something of a cultural reactionary. This hardly matters, since Shakespeare and even Milton (despite Johnson's strong prejudice against Milton) caused Johnson to overthrow his own critical speculations. Boswell is most Johnson's disciple when he is most empirical. He reimagines Johnson by adopting Johnson's own realism. Johnson is a biographical literary critic, and M. J. C. Hodgart was accurate when he observed that "Johnson's short lines are the model for Boswell's concept of 'total' biography. Johnson has the ability to relate everything to his own experience of life, and to identify himself closely with the men he writes about, sharing their problems and emotions."

Boswell too has this ability, even if his close indentification was primarily only with Johnson. That identification, an act of love, is at the center of the *Life of Johnson*. In the many-sided Boswell, this identification is necessarily dialectical, and yet it remains an identification. Every kind of high literary art comes together in the *Life of Johnson*, but the coming together is conditioned and refined by a human love. What finally persuades us in the *Life* is not technique and not even the defense of culture, though Johnson himself exalted both. What persuades us is the elaboration, through adornment, variation, and refinement, of Boswell's surpassing admiration and reverence, of his love for Johnson.

Literary Form in Factual Narrative: The Example of Boswell's *Johnson*

Ralph W. Rader

Although factual narrative, that is to say, history and biography, is certainly an art, only a few biographies and histories are unequivocally literature. This paradox deserves explanation and will in fact provide the whole subject of my remarks in this chapter. While much biography and history has a clear if relatively low place in literature, only Boswell and Gibbon in English have constructed factual narratives which stand unquestioned as literary masterpieces of the very first rank. On the other hand, much excellent biography and history has no place in literature at all. The explanation for these facts lies in the fundamental contrast between the fictional and the factual narrative modes. Literature in general is, in Coleridge's phrase, that species of composition which proposes pleasure rather than truth as its immediate object. The purely literary artist is free to invent, dispose, weight, and vivify his materials as a means to the greatest intensity of effect, whereas the immediate object of the biographer or historian cannot be effect but fidelity to truth.

Some works of history and biography nevertheless produce a distinct and powerful effect closely akin to those which characterize works of the imagination, and these of course are, as they should be from Coleridge's definition, the very works which rank as literature.

But though we speak of Gibbon's epical sweep and force and Macaulay's dramatic powers, we ought not to succumb to the temptations of analogy and talk as if the *Decline and Fall* were in fact an epic, or the *History of England* a drama, or even as if the most celebrated contemporary work of factual narrative is what its author calls it, a nonfiction novel. To do so would be to evade the terms of the question we want to answer, which is, not how literary works are literary, but how works whose primary commitment is distinctly nonliterary nevertheless become literature.

The answer which I am going to propose is that such works become literature by transcending while fulfilling the usual purpose of history and biography, to provide true knowledge of the human past. I am going to suggest that factual narratives in order to compass a literary effect must raise their subjects constructively out of the past and represent them to the imagination as concrete, self-intelligible causes of emotion. My claim will be that these works of history thereby become, paradoxically, "a more philosophical and a higher thing than history." They become universal, in Aristotle's sense, because they are displayed to the imagination not as contingent but as concretely probable, and valuable in terms of that general human nature which as human beings we all share and intuitively know. I choose as my text Boswell's *Life of Johnson* but shall return intermittently and at the close to a view of the overall subject.

It has not been obvious to the authors of the two most extensive and scholarly modern treatments of biography that the greatest work of factual narrative in our language has a structure which is the cause of its greatness, and that effective structure, as all writers should know, is never an accident. Donald Stauffer, though he gives high praise to Boswell's artistry, says flatly that "the structure of the *Life* is open to serious question." It lacks narrative connection and temporal development, it fails to scale itself to the proportions of Johnson's life, and (astoundingly) it fails to create Johnson, affording rather "materials from which Johnson may be created by an imaginative act." John Garraty repeats the charges and adds a few of his own: the book is "all out of proportion"; it is merely "one man's recollections of another"; it lacks "not so much unity as cumulative effect and a comprehensive estimate of its subject and his importance." As we shall see, it would make as much sense to blame Shakespeare for not providing a comprehensive estimate of Hamlet. Most of these criticisms point to real facts about the substance and structure of the *Life*, but they do not point to faults. Only the inadequate theoretical conception which underlies the criticism could make these facts seem faults, for no reader intuitively reacts to them as such. The problem lies in conceiving Boswell's work as if it were an ordinary explanatory narrative, like Krutch's biography of Johnson. If it were such a biography, then it would be a manifestly defective one, and we should have to pronounce it inferior to Krutch's. This would be absurd, for fine as it is, Krutch's biography is not great literature and Boswell's is. That is the whole point. It is literature. It is not an explanatory narrative but an emotive narrative of the type we have indicated, one whose whole principle is not to give instrumental information and explanation but rather to reconstruct and present as concrete and universal an aspect of human fact so as to render it inherently the cause of a distinct effect. What aspect of fact does Boswell reconstruct, and what is its effect? The answer lies in the last sentence of his book: "Such was Samuel Johnson, a man whose talents, acquirements, and virtues were so extraordinary, that the more his character is considered, the more he will be regarded by the present age and by posterity, with admiration and reverence." The subject of Boswell's book is not the life of Johnson but the *character* of Johnson as revealed in the facts of his life; and his purpose is to make us feel that admiration and reverence which is the natural emotive consequence of full empathetic perception of the character.

Unlike Scott's life, Johnson's career as a connected sequence of actions could not have been presented as the cause of a powerful effect. It is his character alone—the extraordinary strength, subtlety, and depth of his mental powers, joined with the nobility and magnanimity of his moral nature and his astonishing powers of expression—that contains the potentiality of such an effect. This Boswell knew. That concluding sentence is no accident, nor is the brilliant character sketch which precedes it and pulls together into a single retrospective view the subject which the myriad pieces of his book have together evoked.

Character must be manifested in the concrete, and Johnson's character is known primarily from its concrete manifestations in the *Life*. Just because the concrete is or seems to be a given reality, however, Boswell has gained small credit for showing it to us. So discerning a critic as Joseph Wood Krutch can see Boswell's technique as wholly naturalistic: "What he [needs is] not imagination or insight, or even, primarily, the judgment to select. It is documentation and more documentation." The well-known, often answered, but still recurring charge that Boswell was nothing but a tape recorder is a ghost that ought to be permanently laid, but it will continue to haunt us until we perceive with more clarity and certainty than we yet have that Boswell's book is, in the part and in the whole, not a recording of fact but always and everywhere an implicitly affecting artistic selection and construction of an aspect of fact. George Mallory pointed out long ago that the effect of the *Life* does not depend on its factuality but upon Boswell's power of "picking out [from the facts] all that was characteristic and important, of ruthlessly discarding unnecessary details and presenting only the salient points." "He gives not the whole of Johnson's words but the essence of them," preserving only "the spirit [and, we may add, the effect] of Johnson's talk and the atmosphere of the moment as the listeners felt it." The talk is "too deliberate, too close, too well-winnowed, as it were" to be a transcript of the actual. The effect of Boswell's operation on the facts, Mallory nevertheless concludes, was to make the whole more real, "a better representation of Johnson."

All this implies the creative secret of Boswell's art: he had within his mind not a series of disjunctive photographic impressions but a single dynamic image of Johnson which, though it derived from innumerable manifestations of Johnson's character, was nevertheless quite independent of any particular manifestation and even independent of their sum. He knew Johnson's image mimetically, and he knew it in its essence. We remember that he could impersonate Johnson more vividly and exactly than Garrick, giving something that approached a full psychosomatic impression. We remember that he could make fresh Johnsoniana, with the ring of the true coin: "Dine with Jack Wilkes, Sir! I'd as soon dine with Jack Ketch!" But just because he possessed Johnson's image so completely within himself, he knew its value immediately and fully through the involuntary psychic comparison with himself which the act of mimetic participation implied. In Johnson's presence Boswell always felt an intense exhilaration as he imaginatively participated in Johnson's powers. It is easy to understand how in retrospect that exhilaration became an unshakable reverence and admiration.

In creating the *Life*, then, Boswell was in a real sense creating an objective correlative of a grand emotive idea. His idea was not so much an aid to him in his task as it was the very principle of that astonishing reconstruction. No other assumption can account for the fact, indicated by Mallory and others, that the Johnson of the *Life* is more Johnsonian than Johnson himself could invariably be. To breathe life into the concentrated dust of the notes and to shape from them the form of the living Johnson can in no sense be conceived as a mechanical act directed toward a string of discrete memories but only as a fully organic act of the creative imagination. Boswell had not to record dead memories but to construct a re-enactment of Johnson which would be concretely adequate in itself to reproduce and release in the reader the emotion which the living man had once produced in him. And the fullest proof of the truly imaginative nature of his act is that he found the correlative of his idea not only in the facts which he himself had witnessed but in all the other facts which his industry had brought to light. His book, he says, is made up of "innumerable detached particulars," but it is not therefore a melange; the particulars are not a heterogeneous collection of facts but a homogeneous presentation of character. Each of the particulars is displayed by Boswell, to the degree which each inherently permits, as an epiphany of an infinitely varied but always single character. Boswell's image of Johnson is the selective, constructive, and controlling principle of the *Life*, the omnipresent element which vivifies and is made vivid in the whole. The image is the unity—the real and living unity—of the *Life*.

It is obvious therefore why the book lacks narrative connection and temporal development. The uniqueness of Johnson's character manifested itself in moments of time and not over a temporal sequence. There is no external connection of parts in the *Life* because the subject can be expressed only as the essence of its individual manifestations; there is no development because the character *in its uniqueness* was static. It is obvious also why the book is not scaled to the proportions of the actual life: more facts expressive of character were available from the late than from the early life.

The creative and unifying role which Boswell's internalized idea of Johnson plays in the *Life* can be forcefully demonstrated from his treatment of those portions of the life in which he himself had played no part. Critics have not sufficiently noticed the very many occasions when Boswell shows his dramatic talent quite independent of his memory. One recalls, for example, the vivid and pleasing scene where Langton and Beauclerk rouse a comically formidable Johnson in the middle of the night and take him on a midnight frisk. It is alive before us; yet Boswell was a boy in Edinburgh when it occurred. How many such scenes in the *Life* Boswell never saw but makes the reader see because he saw them not in reality but where the true artist always sees—in the mind's eye. But of the parts in which Boswell's memory played no part, the most instructive for our present purpose are those which may be compared with parallel parts from the works of Boswell's rivals, Hawkins and Mrs. Piozzi. Neither of those writers, of course, was moved by any detached sense of Johnson's magnificent mystery to discover every possible sign of it; they were content with what lay at hand. The very immensity of Boswell's *Life* is itself evidence, in comparison with their works, of the way in which he was possessed by the essence of his subject and motivated to give it body. They were prompted to write about a particular man whom they had known, from private emotion; Boswell was driven to write about a man who was intrinsically of interest to all men, by disinterested universal emotion. Both Hawkins and Mrs. Piozzi held and expressed the same general estimate of Johnson that Boswell does—he was an astonishingly great and good man—but neither is consistently able to show us the materials of their works as the cause of their estimate. Too often, they allow merely personal feeling to interfere with their presentation of the universal Johnson. Consider the following anecdote told by both Boswell and Mrs. Piozzi. Boswell first:

> In the playhouse at Lichfield, as Mr. Garrick informed me, Johnson having for a moment quitted a chair which was placed for him between the side-scenes, a gentleman took possession of it, and when Johnson on his return civilly demanded his seat, rudely refused to give it up; upon which Johnson laid hold of it, and tossed him and the chair into the pit.

Mrs. Piozzi's version is as follows: Garrick "said that in their young days, when some strolling players came to Lichfield, our friend had fixed his place upon the stage, and got himself a chair accordingly; which leaving a few minutes, he found a man in it at his return, who refused to give it back at the first intreaty: Mr. Johnson, however, who did not think it worth his while to make a second, took chair and man and all together and threw them all at once into the pit." There is a good deal of difference in precision and elegance of narration here, of course; Boswell's is much the shorter, with no irrelevant detail, the whole laid out in the clean curve of a single sentence. And Boswell's works together with a series of short epiphanies he is giving at the moment to illustrate his nicely discriminated immediate thesis that Johnson was afraid of nothing but death, not even what might occasion death. But the most basic difference is that Boswell's version in itself supports his claim that Johnson was a great and good man. Mrs. Piozzi's does not support her claim and thereby fails to display that which she has pointed to as the natural interest of her subject. The choice which she made in evaluating Garrick's story was as a personal moral choice just as justifiable as Boswell's, but as an artistic choice, it was not defensible at all, since it diminished the inherent potential of the subject. If Johnson had been as she shows him here, we would feel no interest and take no pleasure in reading about him. Mrs. Piozzi's mistake was repeated, on a much larger scale, by a much greater biographer—Froude, in his *Life of Carlyle*.

There is an example of parallel tendency in Hawkins, who writes thus of a famous incident at Oxford: Johnson had

> scarce any change of raiment, and, in a short time after Corbet left him, but one pair of shoes, and those so old, that his feet were seen through them: a gentleman of his college, the father of an

eminent clergyman now living, directed a servitor one morning
to place a new pair at the door of Johnson's chamber, who, seeing
them upon his first going out, so far forgot himself and the spirit
that must have actuated his unknown benefactor, that, with all
the indignation of an insulted man, he threw them away.

The essential facts are as Boswell is to present them: the shoes were given
and Johnson was indignant. The problem is in evaluation: it was a fault in
Johnson to be indignant. It may be true; yet in judging Johnson on a narrow
moral base Hawkins diminishes him. Johnson is seen to fall away from a
universal standard of virtue and to become by that much less the man because
of whose greatness Hawkins is writing. Boswell, without at all changing the
facts, reads and relates them in a much different way:

> Mr. Bateman's lectures were so excellent, that Johnson used to
> come and get them at second-hand from Taylor, till his poverty
> being so extreme, that his shoes were worn out, and his feet
> appeared through them, he saw that this humiliating circumstance
> was perceived by the Christ-Church men, and he came no more.
> He was too proud to accept of money, and somebody having set
> a pair of new shoes at his door, he threw them away with
> indignation. How must we feel when we read such an anecdote
> of Samuel Johnson!

Hawkins' inert details and judgments drop out as Boswell makes us feel
Johnson's poverty and the reality of his consequent humiliation. Boswell
construed his pride convincingly as a sign of his majestic independence, and
suppressing the irrelevant clergyman, evaluates the incident not in relation
to him but to Johnson's essential character and the fact of his permanent
greatness, something to which Bateman's excellent lectures and Johnson's
desire for them are not of course irrelevant. Critics often seem to assume
that the Boswellian record is superior to the Hawkins and Piozzi record
largely in its greater material fullness: there is more documentation. If this
were true, then it would have been no literary crime for Croker to have
conflated as he did all three works together; facts are facts. But it *was* a
crime because the records are different not in extent but, as Professor Clifford
has seen, in their fundamental nature. Boswell's facts are created according
to the model of a living universal idea of a great man, the minor biographers'
as impressions of the contingent acts of a contingent man who sometimes
displayed his greatness.

(The passage quoted from Hawkins, incidentally, witnesses to an interesting point. In attempting to impose universal moral judgment on Johnson's imperfect action, Hawkins is imitating Johnson's own biographical practice, just as he attempted to imitate Johnson's style. Johnson succeeds in his biographies because he genuinely does impose his judgment on the facts. His biographies are literature because they achieve universality of their subject. The pleasure of Johnson's *Lives* is Johnson, not Pope or Addison. This shows how untrue is the usual statement that Boswell followed Johnson's biographical example. He followed it in its emphasis on character and on characterizing particularity, but he departed totally from the basic Johnsonian mode of presentation. Johnson's practice, of course, was ideally suited to his gifts, for the same reasons that made him the ideal subject for Boswell's kind of biography.)

Once the nature of Boswell's image of Johnson has been pointed out, its presence and constructive function are everywhere apparent. Many facts in the *Life*, however, would not in themselves contribute directly to our vivid sense of the character, and it is not immediately clear why they should have been included if the subject of the work is as I describe it. Briefly we may say that Boswell treats the full range of facts in the *Life* on the assumption, amply born out by modern scholars, that anything connected with such a man will contribute a little bit more to our attempt to fill out and confirm the inherently fascinating reality of his image. In factual literature, we *do* want to know how many children had Lady Macbeth. But Boswell, as may easily be illustrated, always proportions his treatment of a fact to the relevance it has for the image of essential character, so that he dismisses quickly much that has great importance in the progress of Johnson's life and devotes pages to what does not affect its progress at all. He explains the substantive biographical facts adequately as facts but always in such a way as to shape and control their significance as emblems of the admirable character. Take, for instance, Boswell's account of Johnson's pension. We see at once that it is not an account of a fact in itself but a transformation of a potentially hostile fact into the terms of the image. He begins by placing the grant in the glowing context of George III's liberal and disinterested patronage and only then contemptuously characterizes the charges of venality which had been made against Johnson. He then refutes the charges by a detailed citation of witnesses, painstakingly and concretely recreating the motivation on both sides, and emerges with the dramatically won conclusion that the pension had been granted on "liberal and honourable terms." The passage closes with Johnson's nobly dignified letter to Bute, which concretely confirms and amplifies the judgment Boswell has offered so that the reader is left secure in truth and admiration, the image not only intact but fortified. Examples of such essay-parts, as we may call them, clearly shaped to the large end of the book, could be multiplied.

But the fact that the shaping role of Boswell's grand image of Johnson is especially obvious in particular passages should not prevent our perceiving its active presence in every part of the *Life*. We hear it vibrate in the fanfare of the very first sentence: "To write the Life of him who excelled all mankind in writing the lives of others, and who, whether we consider his extraordinary endowments, or his various works, has been equalled by few in any age, is an arduous, and may be reckoned in me a presumptuous task." A grand and confident claim has been made upon our attention. We necessarily infer that the claim has a cause in reality external to the narrator, and we respond as to a perceived fact with a corresponding mental and emotional assumption of our own. The narrative posture thereafter continuously asserts the real existence of the image thus evoked and continues to demand its counterpart in us. Thus, even when the facts immediately produced do not actively validate the image, the reader never doubts its reality because the narrator does not evaluate such facts as validation but only as necessarily interesting and relevant, in relation to the curiosity which the continuing image naturally generates.

More than narrative assertion is required, of course, to call Johnson's spirit from the vasty deep, particularly in the opening pages where so little of the concrete is available; and the discerning critic can only admire the many subtle means Boswell employs to bring the permanent Johnson quickly before us. In the facts of the youth he discovers the greatness of the man; and with the voice of the man he makes the youth vivid. He selects, compresses, dramatizes, vivifies to such a degree that when at last the figure of Johnson walks through Davies' doorway, he is an old and beloved acquaintance.

More largely, throughout the *Life*, many subtle features, quite distinct from its factual substance, conspire to renew and intensify our sense of the grandeur of the subject. Recurring epithets like "my illustrious friend" give us a tug of pleasure and reanimate our established estimate as we think subconsciously, "he *was* illustrious." Even such apparently irrelevant aspects of the book as its praise of great men, or its literary allusions, or Boswell's digression on the qualities of a noble estate contribute in the aggregate to the massive special effect of the whole. (Only consider how much grander and more spacious is the world of the *Life* than the world of Boswell's *London Journal*.)

In a moment I shall pay detailed attention to the means by which the image is given redundant concrete specification, but I should not leave the subject of the peripheral means Boswell employs in connection with it without noticing two directly related matters, his citation of the testimony of others and his use of Johnson's letters. Both these dimensions of his work serve as necessary guarantees that we are encountering not a personal but a universal view of the subject. The testimony of others validates and extends the view Boswell himself takes; and the letters, each of which, as Professor Daghlian has recently noted, powerfully images Johnson's noble character, offer the strongest possible objective corroboration of the image: the Johnson we meet in the letters is indubitably the same as the Johnson Boswell elsewhere shows us. From all this we understand how the image becomes a covert but omnipresent reality in the *Life*, even in those facts which in themselves would not evoke it. The explanation offered here as confined by the actual experience of a continuous reading of the *Life* allows us to understand how such seemingly inert facts are drawn into relevance by the unseen lines of magnetic force which the large image and emotional flow of the whole exert and how each functions as one of the myriad particles which together make the lines real and distinct. The image constructs the facts, and the facts in turn construct the image; the process, circular and progressive, constitutes the linear coherence and material unity of the *Life*.

But unity and coherence do not by themselves make literature. To understand why the *Life* is a supremely literary work, we must explain its power, unmatched among factual narratives, of producing literary pleasure. The explanation lies in the unusual degree to which the *Life* is able, within the limits of truth, to meet Coleridge's supplementary requirement that literary works ought to be so designed as to give in each of their parts as much pleasure as is consonant with the greatest pleasure in the whole. Lockhart's *Life of Scott*, for instance, has a plot-like structure, a single line of developing tragic perception, which produces a powerful single effect, but the constituent parts are relatively inert. As a whole, consequently, it is much less a work of literature than Boswell's. The *Life of Johnson* gives maximum pleasure just because it is so preponderantly made up of images of Johnson's acts, each of which has its own particular pleasure which, when most fully realized, most contributes to the peculiar pleasure of the whole. To understand this, we must remember what Aristotle teaches: that literary pleasure results from the vivid representation to our consciousness of striking human acts, morally determinate, which move us through our perception of the internal probability and ethical consonance of their inception, continuance, and completion. Now, as I shall more fully illustrate, all the acts in the *Life* are represented according to this formula. Boswell renders them vivid and striking, makes us see them as internally probable in terms of motive and circumstance, and adjusts our view so that we always see them as ethically consonant both in themselves and with the morally determinate image of an admirable Johnson. Each of the representational parts, then, has its own local pleasure, but the parts are of such a nature that in sum they also form the basis of the larger literary pleasure of the entire book—the single continuing, growing and self-reinforcing pleasure of encountering in new and striking but always probable manifestations the astonishing character of Samuel Johnson. That we know these new manifestations as probable and encounter them with anticipatory expression, nontheless exists as an active essence in the reader's mind which, as I have already said, effectively renders even the inert parts concrete. (That we possess the liberated image of Johnson even after the fact of reading the *Life* is demonstrated by the effect upon us of the words "Sir" or "Why, No Sir" spoken out of context but with appropriate inflection. The utterance immediately brings to mind that amusing but admirable conjunction of sincere deference and rational aggression which together reflect the essence of Johnson's character. A similar phenomenon obtains for no other historical figure.)

It may help to clarify the large structural principle of the *Life* if we recall that we have already seen it in action in the episodes compared with their counterparts in Hawkins and Mrs. Piozzi. When Boswell's Johnson throws the interloper off the stage, we are made to see his action as ethically consonant with, though conventionally disproportionate to, the provocation he has received and his own dignity, so that the scene becomes comically pleasing; at the same time, Johnson's overall moral stature is pleasurably confirmed and reinforced. Mrs. Piozzi's Johnson, by contrast, is neither amusing nor admirable. When Boswell's Johnson throws away the shoes at Oxford, we are moved by a momentary pulse of admiring compassion, because we understand the grounds of his act fully and evaluate it as justified; at the same time, we see a permanently grand aspect of his nature. Hawkins' Johnson is shown to neither purpose.

But Coleridge's principle about the relation of parts to the whole has in view not only such material parts as episodes in a representation but also purely qualitative parts. The pleasure of any literary work will increase in proportion as all its elements, including those of language itself—syntax, diction, and pure sound—are arranged so as actively to support the effect. For example, other things being equal, a representation in verse is more intensely pleasing than one in prose. Here, then, is another cause of the supreme literary quality of the *Life*. Johnson's speech—edited and pointed by Boswell to preserve and heighten its Johnsonian essence—makes him the only character in factual literature whose speech is equal to or superior to that of fictional characters. The graceful elasticity and full vital expressiveness of Boswell's own purposefully unobtrusive style work toward the same end to make the *Life* unique as a factual work which to the large pleasure of concrete character and the smaller pleasure of concrete act can add the fully perfecting concrete pleasures of language itself. (At least once in the *Life* we get the pleasure of speech as a pure increment to the already forceful sense: "He seemed to take pleasure in speaking in his own style," says Boswell, "for when he had carelessly missed it, he would repeat the thought translated into it. Talking of the Comedy of 'The Rehearsal,' he said, 'It has not wit enough to keep it sweet.' This was easy; he therefore caught himself, and pronounced a more rounded sentence; 'It has not vitality enough to preserve it from putrefaction.' " Pure style, pure pleasure—but as always in Johnson, the style is the man.)

But the vital corpuscles of the *Life's* body are the acts. Let us take them first at their simplest and then at their most complex. The simplest kind of complete act represented in the *Life* is an aphorism or generalization by Johnson without context. Now any general truth even independent of a speaker has a representational character and force: the mind perceives it as a self-caused, inherently purposeful, surprising but probable act of cognition, carrying with it therefore its own distinct pleasure. The pleasure of a generalization will be greater in proportion to the degree in which it is both true and unobvious, to the inherent human relevance of its substance, and to the concision and force of its expression. To describe the conditions of pleasure in generalizations is to suggest the qualities of Johnson's. As much as La Rochefoucauld's and Pascal's, Johnson's sayings have literary value in and of themselves, with the additional pleasure of their spontaneity; it is not too much to say that the recorded impromptus of all other men together do not equal the total of his in pleasure and value. Yet all of his remarks in the *Life* give additional pleasure, on the large grounds sketched out above, in that they satisfy as fresh but unforseeable signs of the power of the character and at the same time add an increment to the total pleasurable image. Let us take one of the myriad examples, the statement, "All censure of a man's self is oblique praise. It is in order to show how much he can spare. It has all the invidiousness of self-praise, and all the reproach of falsehood." The initial sentence, paradoxical and surprising, is quickly and pleasingly rendered inherently probable (that is, true) by the explanatory second sentence. The compelling analytic judgment of the third sentence converts what might have been a cynicism of La Rochefoucauld's into an implicit positive base of moral operations. It is not directed scornfully at *other* men but put instructively, for the use of *all* men, including the speaker. The statement surprises, pleases, and teaches; and it leaves the mind with a renewed and augmented sense of the simultaneously good, wise, and articulate man who made it. But even when Johnson's statements are perfectly particular they are pleasurable merely as fresh revelations of the established admirable character. "Sir, I would walk to the extent of the diameter of the earth to save Beauclerk." Or: "Sir, you have not travelled over *my* mind, I promise you." Notice that the hyperbolical first statement would not please if our conviction of Johnson's majestic rectitude and the depth of his feeling did not give it substance; and that the second, if said by Goldsmith to Johnson, rather than the other way around, would be merely an egotistical impertinence.

But the most massively pleasing parts of the *Life* are its scenes. The art of the major scenes is so plain that they have often drawn praise upon Boswell for the vividness of their pointing and their parenthetical stage directions ["Johnson (puffing and blowing): . . ."]. But these praises are often analytically empty because the critics who give them have no conception of the form and effect to which the devices are subordinate. After "vivid" and "dramatic" there is nothing left. Space does not permit me to work in full detail through the most famous scene in the *Life*, the Wilkes episode, but a partial analysis can sufficiently demonstrate how much its effect depends upon Boswell's handling. Its essential structure may be described by expanding the basic formula already set down: it is a full Aristotelian action which follows the predicament of a central character from a beginning which defines the terms of that predicament, through a middle which develops and complicates it and our reactions to the full, to an end which resolves the complications and brings our emotional participation to satisfactory discharge and close. More particularly, it is a comic action. Now in a comic action the hero is of mixed character—essentially and predominantly good, so that we wish him finally well; at the same time flawed or restricted in a way that involves him in embarrassments which are the substance of the complications of the plot. We view these embarrassments with delight both because they are of the hero's own making and because the conduct of the story assures us throughout that he will in some way that our perplexity cannot foresee ultimately achieve the due which his fundamentally good character deserves and that meanwhile nothing really harmful or painful will befall him. Boswell shows us the Wilkes episode according to just this formula.

At the outset, Johnson is already secure in our admiration, but Boswell must make us actively desire to see a kind of trick played on him. He does this initially by making us feel that the meeting will be a delightful experiment in human nature which will end much to the Doctor's credit and by heightening our sense of that awful personal power in Johnson which by itself guarantees the preservation of his dignity while it enhances our comic sense of Boswell's resourceful daring. ("How to manage it, was a nice and difficult matter.") Boswell sets the terms of the story by defining Johnson and Wilkes as "celebrated men" who, though as different as they could possibly be, are yet both friends of Boswell. The meeting is thus neatly characterized as potentially productive either of an explosion or a conciliation. We are made to feel that the last will and ought to be the result but are left to wonder how, considering Johnson's strong moral and political prejudices, the first will be avoided. The terms are quickly sharpened with the apparently gratuitous paragraph about Sir John Pringle who, like Wilkes, was also linked to Johnson through the middle term of Boswell's friendship but who, though an excellent man, was "not sufficiently flexible" to meet agreeably with him. The paragraph has a very precise function: it underlines the potential explosiveness of the desired meeting and Boswell's own underlying assurance that the explosion will somehow not occur, while at the same time it defines any inflexibility which might stand in its way as a regrettable human limitation. From this point on, therefore, the reader must actively hope that Johnson will be able to meet Wilkes on affable terms, while he is all the more aware of the piquant difficulties.

The paragraph on arrangements with Dilly increases with every detail our sense of the necessity that Johnson for his own sake meet the standards of social sophistication, while Dilly's represented alarm reinforces our sense of the internal barrier to his doing so. The next scene shows Boswell with consummate meekness and guile inducing Johnson to accept the invitation through a subtle challenge to his vanity as a social man. The paragraph could sustain a page of analysis, but I will only say that its brilliance consists in Boswell's heightening our comic sense of Johnson's majestically cantankerous nature at the same time that he makes us sympathetic to Johnson's full if inadvertent commitment of his pride to the fact that he is not ultimately limited by his prickliness. "And if Jack Wilkes *should* be there, what is that to *me*, Sir?" Johnson must make good this commitment, but all the more we wonder: how is he to do it?

The obstacle presented by Mrs. Williams is used fully by Boswell to heighten by opposing the wishes we have formed to see the meeting take place, as well as for other purposes; and when the obstacle is overcome we exult with Boswell as his prize is carried off. Snug and silent, we watch with delight the impact upon Johnson of Mr. Arthur Lee and then Mr. Wilkes. Boswell defines Lee's comic function with brilliant economy by juxtaposing a description of him in the idiom of Johnson's prejudice—he was both a "patriot" and an "American"—with a comment that underlines his membership in the civilized world of which we desire Johnson to be fully a member—Lee was, Boswell says, later American ambassador to the Court of Madrid. In other words, we see Lee at once as Johnson in his comic limitation sees him and also as he really is and as Johnson must therefore finally accept him if he is to maintain and increase our regard. But just at this moment we are most aware of the resources it will require in Johnson to overcome the strength of his prejudice as Boswell vividly communicates his comic distress—"too, too, too." The distress is visible, but if the effect is to be maintained, we need as well some assurance that the hoped for if as yet unspecifiable triumph will eventually come and that it will come not accidentally but as a result of Johnson's deliberate attempt to master himself and the situation. No sign is available, and so Boswell boldly goes into Johnson's mind to get it for us: "His feelings, *I dare say*, were awkward enough. But he *no doubt* recollected his having rated me for supposing that he could be at all disconcerted by any company, and he, *therefore*, resolutely set himself to behave quite as an easy man of the world, who could adapt himself at once to the disposition and manners of those whom he might chance to meet." The sympathetic vanity and our hopes for its triumph are strong in our minds.

Despite his resolution, Johnson's "surly virtue" is shown to yield only gradually as the conciliatory gestures of the suave but sincere Wilkes make us wish all the more for Johnson's triumph of sophistication. All the matter now heightens and foreshadows the climax, in ways we cannot pause to notice, until we get the climactic interchange: "JOHNSON (to Mr. Wilkes) 'You must know, Sir, I lately took my friend Boswell and shewed him genuine civilised life in an English provincial town. I turned him loose at Litchfield, my native city, that he might see for once real civility: for you know he lives among savages in Scotland, and among rakes in London.' WILKES. 'Except when he is with grave, sober, decent people like you and me.' JOHNSON, (smiling) 'And we ashamed of him.'" The speeches please not just in themselves but because they resolve with such unexpected and delightful fulness the underlying tensions which have been so clearly and vividly represented from the outset. Johnson's first speech — "and rakes in London"—

covertly and politely acknowledges and thus neutralizes the antagonism which he has felt toward Wilkes and which has been the source of our comic concern. Wilkes, just as politely, denies any antagonism by defining himself with Johnson as among the "grave, sober, decent people"—the three adjectives are a giveaway—as opposed to the rakes. Johnson's smiling "And we ashamed of him" accepts the denial, cancels the animosity, joins himself to Wilkes, and, in a complete reversal of the original terms of the incident, leaves the Boswell who had challenged Johnson's civility comically out in the social cold, a barbarous Scot. The single adjective, "smiling," applied to Johnson is, of course, not just a piece of random vividness but is crucially important to our full sense of the active benevolence with which Johnson reconciles himself to Wilkes; it is not the limited triumph of self-control over ineradicable and debilitating prejudice, but the full-hearted triumph of a capaciously human soul whose prejudice is only a temporary defect of its large virtues. It should be clear even from this brief analysis that the pleasurable effect not only of the climax but of the whole depends on the fact *only* as they are selected, revealed and evaluated by Boswell's art.

The interchange does not end the episode, but we cannot pause to follow Boswell's means of bringing it to full aesthetic completeness. Enough has been said to show how the episode, like the other parts we have examined, makes its fullest contribution to the overall purpose of the *Life* when its own appropriate pleasure is most realized. The inherent particular effect of the Wilkes episode is comic pleasure, and that pleasure has been seen to increase in proportion to Johnson's triumph. The greater, the more surprising, and yet characteristically probable the triumph, the greater the comic pleasure. But obviously then the greater the comic pleasure, the greater our residual admiration for Johnson. We should notice, too, that the episode necessarily depends on the preceding part of the *Life*, for an active idea of Johnson's character is a requisite of its comic effect. No one who reads the episode without experience of the *Life* will think it very funny.

A great part of the pleasure of the scenes taken as a whole is their wide range of effect from somberness to the gayest lightness, while all express the same Johnson and all are indebted to Boswell's art. Consider, for instance, the grand scene where Boswell introduces "the subject of death, and [endeavors] to maintain that the fear of it might be got over." The conversation must have lasted some time but Boswell gives only its heart. Johnson's defense of his own fear of death as against the alleged lack of fear in Hume and Foote justifies him immediately in our estimation because he finds evidence for his own feelings that we cannot deny: "Hold a pistol to

Foote's breast, or to Hume's breast, and threaten to kill them, and you'll see how they behave." Still, we would not be really prepared to absorb the gigantic outburst which follows Boswell's "But may we not fortify our minds for the approach of death?" if Boswell had not been able, without breaking the rhythm of the scene, to specify and ennoble Johnson's inner state:

> I am sensible I was in the wrong, to bring before his view what he ever looked upon with horrour; for although when in a celestial frame, in his "Vanity of human wishes," he has supposed death to be "kind Nature's signal for retreat," from this state of being to "a happier seat," his thoughts upon this aweful change were in general full of dismal apprehensions. His mind resembled the vast amphitheatre, the Coliseum at Rome. In the centre stood his judgement, which, like a mighty gladiator, combated those apprehensions that, like the wild beasts of the *Arena*, were all around in cells, ready to be let out upon him. After a conflict, he drove them back into their dens; but not killing them, they were still assailing him. To my question, whether we might not fortify our minds for the approach of death, he answered, in a passion, "No, Sir, let it alone. It matters not how a man dies, but how he lives. The act of dying is not of importance, it lasts so short a time." He added, (with an earnest look) "A man knows it must be so, and submits. It will do him no good to whine."

Boswell's grand simile, though necessary, is dangerous. Were it not for its manifest accuracy and truth and its immediate validation by the grandeur of Johnson's reply, so artificial a comparison could easily have been a disaster. But it succeeds by forcing us to understand that Johnson's unusual fear of death does not diminish him, since it makes us feel how constant and tremendous the pressures upon him were, how great was the effort needed to hold them in equilibrium, and how near to breaking without ever really breaking his majestic nature was. The agitated but noble reply confirms all this and releases Johnson from the blame of personal defect because, though it functions fully as the sign to us of his particular emotion, it is perfectly general and fully applicable to all other human beings, so that we see him not as a particular fearful man but as an exemplar of the most basic kind of human heroism. Our sense of the splendid agony of his bravery carries over to his full credit as Boswell goes on to tell of his "Give us no more of this" and of his expressing himself "in a way that alarmed and distressed me." When the peremptory "Don't let us meet tomorrow" comes, we feel

not that Johnson has been blamably irritable but only that we have seen a
nature, like ours but much grander, unintentionally provoked beyond
endurance. Boswell, of course, had at the moment been himself made
"extremely uneasy." "All the harsh observations which I had ever heard
made upon his character, crowded into my mind." But in retrospect the
causes of this uneasiness had faded away, irrelevant to the grand epiphany
to which he had been witness, and we ourselves actively perceive only the
universality and not the contingency of the occasion.

But Boswell can preserve not merely the grand essential moments but
also the very small ones. It is sometimes said that he does not show us the
light, trifling Johnson we know from Burney and Thrale, but consider the
following vignette:

> Johnson was prevailed with to come sometimes into these [blue-
> stocking] circles, and did not think himself too grave even for
> the lively Miss Monckton (now Countess of Corke), who used
> to have the finest *bit of blue* at the house of her mother, Lady
> Galway. Her vivacity enchanted the Sage, and they used to talk
> together with all imaginable ease. A singular instance happened
> one evening, when she insisted that some of Sterne's writings were
> very pathetick. Johnson bluntly denied it. "I am sure (said she)
> they have affected *me*."—"Why, (said Johnson, smiling, and
> rolling himself about,) that is, because, dearest, you're a dunce."
> When she some time afterwards mentioned this to him, he said
> with equal truth and politeness; "Madam, if I had thought so,
> I certainly should not have said it."

Boswell's quick definition of the established mutual regard of the two, the
brief glimpse we get of Johnson's usually ominous tendency to roughness
("bluntly denied") joined to the surprising adroitness and sophistication of
his immediate and ultimate responses to Miss Monckton's momentary and
fetching vulnerability conspire to make the little scene extremely pleasing.
Even so, however, the immediate response would not have given much
pleasure if Boswell had not marked Johnson's inner spirit so accurately by
his description of the Doctor's physical posture. The language ("dearest")
and the movements together wonderfully communicate the delighted
premeditation and benign condescension with which the ponderous Johnson
makes his affectionate thrust. And so Boswell reveals another aspect,
surprising but entirely consonant, of Johnson's astonishing being.

Despite his intention of evoking consistent admiration and reverence for Johnson, Boswell as we have already seen does not suppress our sense of his faults. Boswell set out to write "not his panegyric, which must be all praise, but his Life; which, great and good as he was, must not be supposed to be entirely perfect." Boswell did not suppress faults but deliberately included them and thereby induced Fanny Burney's fear, already noticed, that the portrait of Johnson with all his blemishes would lessen him forever in the eyes of posterity. But Boswell knew that without the blemishes the portrait would not be true and concretely convincing. Unless the reader were to see an image which in its basic structure corresponded to his own imperfect nature, he would not recognize either the paradigmatic likeness or the particular otherness that are the essence of biographical portraiture; he would not admire because he would not believe. Besides, to be as Johnson was, with all his defects, constituted, as Boswell says, "panegyric enough to any man in this state of nature." But Boswell had an artistic motive even higher than verisimilitude for his honesty. He can make Johnson even more admirable by showing that he was so in *spite* of his faults and uglinesses. As in all art, the greater the ugliness overcome, the greater the ultimate beauty and pleasure. As Hume showed long ago, any emotion arising from the contemplation of a painful object is, in the presence of a predominant sentiment of beauty, converted into the higher feeling. Any emotive reaction to faults or ugliness is overcome consistently in Boswell by the emotion attaching to our immediate or residual impression of Johnson's essential greatness and goodness. When Mrs. Piozzi tells us that Johnson was a "gross feeder," the brief image is ugly and painful, while a much more particular and materially ugly description of Johnson's eating by Boswell is not. Mrs. Piozzi's description images her own disgust, Boswell's a more complex but affirmative reaction which assimilates our perception of the intense passion with which Johnson eats to our sense of the gigantic will which drives his being and which does not, except in indifferent matters, break through his moral control. Consistently in the *Life*, as in most of the episodes we have examined, faults are pleasurably rendered as temporary foibles or necessary defects of the great virtues, while the fully represented physical grotesqueness, the eccentricity and ugliness, ultimately serve only to make Johnson's achievement the more concretely real, particular and astonishing.

But even when Johnson's defects cannot be converted to immediately sympathetic pleasure, Boswell faces them directly, in order to show, we may say, how much Johnson can spare. He makes little defense, for instance, of *Taxation No Tyranny*. Johnson should not have written it, and Boswell quotes with approval two animadversions on the pamphlet. Both of these, however, share with Boswell the assumption that the work is an uncharacteristic and unworthy product of the great mind which produced it, and when Boswell goes on to indicate as fully and concretely as he can that Johnson probably shared this view, the effect is complete. Finally, in extreme cases, where Johnson has been excessively rude or violent, Boswell will report an outburst in general terms sufficient to make us understand its character and effect, but not vividly enough to make it actively disagreeable. The most notable example precisely because it is so seldom noted is the occasion when Johnson attacks Boswell himself so fiercely that Boswell is angry for days and almost goes away to Scotland without seeing the Doctor again. The shock was obviously nearly traumatic to Boswell, and affected him personally more deeply perhaps than all but a few of the scenes in the *Life*. His handling of it is characteristic: he *tells* us accurately the substance and effect of Johnson's rudeness, but he does not *show* it to us; in the sequel, however, he dramatizes the reconciliation with great particularity and happy effect. Despite his personal investment, he proportions the weight he gives the scene strictly to its relative value as a sign of his subject—Johnson's character as it is of interest to all men, not Johnson's character as it might appear momentarily to and affect one man. Boswell sees not for himself but for all of us; his book is by no means "one man's recollections of another."

This brings us to our final topic in the *Life*: the general matter of its truth. Most students have emphasized that the strictest truth is essential to biography, but they have meant by truth, ordinarily, authenticity—fidelity to ascertainable empirical fact. The authenticity of Boswell's account has often been investigated and checked against his own records and the records of others. The verdict is nearly unanimous: the *Life* is as authentic as human effort could have made it. Yet we have seen fully characteristic instances when Boswell goes quite beyond the limits of literal truth, as when he dramatizes scenes he has not witnessed, or directly enters Johnson's mind; even the speeches, we have noticed, must be understood as true more in effect than in substance. If, as Johnson himself and many since have insisted, the inherent value of biography depends directly upon its literal truth, how can we justify Boswell's editing, shaping, and evaluation? More generally, how can we explain the fact that we experience the full value of Boswell's book while reading it in complete innocence of all the existing external corroboration of its accuracy? The answer is implicit and to a degree explicit in all that I have been saying. Certified truth in Boswell's book is a requisite as in all factual narrative, but its truth is ultimately relevant not to the external facts of Johnson's life but to the essence of his character; for the book is not about an eighteenth-century man of letters, not about an external life and career, but about a man, significant independent of history, who manifested himself in the events of a life and career. All of Boswell's authenticating assiduity, all the innumerable certified details, are valuable finally not as they give us true external facts but as evidence of the conjunction of that magnificent image with reality; like Defoe's circumstantiality is not a lie. An inherent part of the pleasure of the character is that it *was* real, and without Boswell's endless certification of what might seem the aesthetically indifferent reality around it, our pleasure in the image could not be as certain and full. Our emotion is toward a timeless image but it is nonetheless an image of fact with location in time and place. Nevertheless the only inherently essential fact of the work is the character; and the truth of the character itself, as we understand by now, is something internal to the *Life* itself. We know intuitively that the character is what it appears to be because it is so complex, so various and astonishing in its endless manifestations and yet so obviously consistent and coherent as a whole that its image could have proceeded from no cause except itself. It is not, as some have sneeringly said, that we know that Boswell could not have invented Johnson; rather we know with the fullest intuitive certainty that no one— not Defoe, not even Shakespeare—could have invented him. No fictional personality appraoches the capacities and complexities of Johnson's. Insofar as the reality of the character is concerned, the book is more compelling than any other evidence of any kind could possibly be. The truth about Johnson's life will change and grow, but the essential truth of his character will never be different from what we feel it to be in Boswell; our residual impression of Johnson must always be such as to produce admiration and reverence. And so we end where we began. Boswell's book is literature because it lifts an aspect of human reality from the contingency of history and displays it as a concrete universal—self-validating, self-intelligible, inherently moving, permanently valuable.

For what we experience finally in the book—and this is the most fundamental source of its literary greatness—is not the sum of Johnson's particular actions but the essence of his character, an essence deeply relevant not to the contingency of history but to the permanence of human nature and therefore immediately to ourselves.

Every man desires to be both bound and free. He desires to be free to express his own deepest passions, and he desires to be bound by the ties of morality and convention that link him to other men in love and respect. It follows from this that he desires at the same time to bind his deepest passions and to break through the internalized restraints of society. His pride requires that he be potent; his dignity requires that he be moral. The powers of most men are unequal to the paradox: dignity suffers when the passionate self breaks down, or corrupts, the moral commitment; or pride is diminished as the self in meeting the commitment succumbs to the seductions of the protean forms of hyprocrisy. Literature in general may be understood as, at bottom, a series of symbolic solutions to this paradox, with success dependent upon the degree to which both its dimensions are satisfied. And Johnson's image is the functional core of a great work of literature because his extraordinarily passionate and powerful being, while fully committed to the restraints of convention, morality, and reason, was yet neither corrupted nor rendered impotent. Perpetually he broke powerfully through the ordinary restraints of convention to express his most primal impulses in vindication of his commitment to convention, morality and reason. He thereby created his dignity and justified his pride on the most general human grounds, so that his image could become for all of us a token of the simultaneous freedom and commitment which is possible to human beings. Symbolically in our imaginative sympathy and actually as an example, that image frees us from the burdens of conventional impotence and falsity— from the rehearsed response, the coward's stance, the liar's quinsy—and restores our dignity, and our pride in ourselves and in the human nature which we share with him. That is why the pleasure of the book is so real and so deep.

Johnson's image is therefore one of the most valuable of our cultural possessions, but without Boswell it would never have been freed from the bondage of time. His book is, as Carlyle said, "a revocation of the edict of Destiny; so that Time shall not utterly, not so soon by several centuries, have dominion over us." Not over Johnson, notice, but over us—who have our stake in Johnson. Boswell's construction of his book was a supremely important artistic act. Because it was so fully artistic, however, it *is* fully real and therefore has seemed to many to manifest no art at all. But it should be clear from what we have said that the *Life of Samuel Johnson* is a great book not because the subject was great or because the biographer was great but because both were great; it was a magnificent literary symbiosis. Johnson was all activity, Boswell all potentiality. He—a truly reverent man, as Carlyle says—filled himself with Johnson's greatness and displayed it to posterity shorn of accident and unblemished by any stain of his own private feeling or immense personal ego. That ego indeed had been deeply wounded in the midst of his task when he learned what Johnson had said of him in his letters to Mrs. Thrale, but this did not at all deflect him from his high purpose.

Johnson, if he had known, would have been more grateful to Boswell than posterity has often been. "Sir, it was generous and noble beyond expectation." But even in his life he was not indifferent to Boswell's devotion. We remember the unusual gesture he made in going with Boswell down to Harwich to see him off to Holland. One of the finest moments in the *Life* is our view of him tarrying on the Harwich pier as the receding Boswell perceives him in the distance, "rolling his majestic frame." The moment is strangely moving, because it triggers in proportion to its slightness such a flood of sentiment, Boswell's two epithets render the for once inarticulate figure a sudden and forceful evocation of all the benevolent affection that our experience as shaped by Boswell has attached to his image. Boswell repaid the Doctor for his kindness. His majestic frame will roll there forever in its particular and universal humanity.

A brief postscript about the relevance of the conception offered here of the form of Boswell's *Johnson* to the general problem of literary form in all factual narratives. We may say first that to the degree that any factual narrative is responded to as literature, its form may be analyzed as inherently the cause of an effect. And insofar as the form has the capacity to produce an effect, it will have raised human fact out of contingency and made it concretely present as a striking but inherently probable manifestation of complete and morally determinate human thought, character or action, individual or collective.

It is this noncontingent, universal quality of narratives like Boswell's and Gibbon's which accounts for the indubitable fact that they remain of timeless value while works dealing with contingent aspects of the same subjects are perpetually superseded and absorbed in new expressions. Both kinds of history depend upon truth, but in different ways. The effect of Gibbon's work, for instance, depends on a very simple and unchanging truth which in no way either limits or is limited by more complex explanatory truths about Rome's fall. The effect depends on the undeniable fact that Rome can be viewed by all human beings as a true high civilization, that it passed out of existence, and that none of the actors in the fall could fully comprehend or in any way prevent it. The fall was striking and necessary and therefore, when presented as Gibbon concretely presents it, inherently moving.

In the highest factual literature, therefore, the conditions of literary success approach those of fictional literature, but we must not therefore confuse the two modes. In fiction, the form must totally subsume the whole matter of the work. In most factual works, even when there is literary intent, a good deal of material must necessarily remain only passively adjusted to the form. When effect in factual works is produced in spite of, rather than through, the facts, as in Strachey's sketch of Dr. Colbatch, the result is brilliant but cheap. Factual literature is inescapably connected with external reality, and in the best factual works a necessary part of our pleasure, as we have seen, comes from feeling that, in Carlyle's phrase, the events related "did in very deed occur." Thus, though the formula is the same, the criterion of imaginative commitment in fiction and fact is different; fact *is* stranger than fiction, and when fact is rendered universally true, it can and ought to claim a benefit from its strangeness and particularity that fiction cannot. But the realms of fiction and fact, so absolutely distinct at their extremities of pure imagination and pure explanation, nevertheless come very close to one another at the point where Shakespeare's history plays, say, and *Paradise Lost* on the one hand—fully concrete but dependent on a presumptive relation to fact—look toward works like *The Prelude* and Boswell's *Johnson* on the other which, though largely concrete, demand acceptance as true fact. And even at the extremes, pure explanation, as in Hume's "On Tragedy," can give concrete pleasure in proportion to its clarity, coherence, concision and native significance, while even the veriest work of the imagination must ultimately be dependent on the facts of human nature and existence. (Johnson himself made the point clearly: "The value of every story depends on its being true. A story is a picture either of an individual or of human nature in general: if it be false, it is a picture of nothing.")

But our present concern is with those works which, clearly factual, are nonetheless clearly literature, We can see now why there are so few such works. Fact is seldom such as to be even the potential cause of universal effects. If the decline of the Roman Empire had not been an inherently grand spectacle, Gibbon could never have made it so and given us the gravely sublime pleasure of perceiving the internal human causes of its inevitable fall. If seventeenth-century England had not really produced a nineteenth-century England that was in some perspectives inherently superior to it, while retaining its heritage and essential values, Macaulay could never have shown us the spectacle that causes the grand pride he makes us feel. And even when the facts are potentially productive of art, the man and the occasion rarely meet. The fully imaginative artist has subjects at any time, but the decline of the Roman Empire was available as literature only to the unique gifts of a man who had inherited the special values and attitudes of a single time and place. So it is also with Macaulay, to say nothing of the miraculous conjunction of Johnson and Boswell, a special providence for which humanity must ever be grateful.

The very great barriers to full literary success in factual narrative are illustrated by Truman Capote's *In Cold Blood*. Here an artist of great capacity seized the accidentally available opportunity and realized it to the full extent of its potentialities. Displaying powers of imaginative reconstruction and synthesis equalled only by Boswell, he yet failed, I believe, to achieve the highest kind of factual literature. Capote does an extraordinary thing. He makes us appreciate the full horror and senseless cruelty of the inexplicable, bloody, night-time murder of a whole family remarkable for its normal decency in a broad social context of normal, uneventful decency, but he makes us feel at the same time a much more unusual thing. He makes us feel for the murderers not anger or a desire for vengeance but rather a peculiar if limited sympathy. The sympathy can be defined by saying that we see Dick's and Perry's actions as the result of their whole nature and lives, for which they are not to blame, and that consequently we do not hate them or desire their deaths; but neither, on the other hand do we feel toward them any real mercy or forgiveness. This effect is the strength but also the limitation of the book. Our failure to feel mercy and forgiveness means that finally we do not recognize Dick and Perry as fully sharing our common nature; we feel that we could not, in any conceivable circumstances, have done what they did. Our intimate knowlege of the murderers widens our view of human existence but it does not make us better able to bear it. The same is true from the point of view of the victims. When Hamlet dies, or when Rome falls, we perceive how human beings are involved in their own necessary destruction, but we feel strongly after the fact that even in the face of destruction it was worthwhile to be Hamlet, worthwhile that Rome was. But the Clutters' death, we are made to see, is a monstrous accident with no moral relevance whatever to them. There is no ethical consonance in it, so that we do not feel retrospectively that it was worthwhile for them to have lived, or that to have lived and died as they did would be worthwhile to us. The whole story offers only a limited catharsis and no residual grandeur. The defect is not in Capote's art, except as it selected the subject, but in the subject itself, inherently defective because not sufficiently universal.

History and biography then cannot often aspire to the purity of Boswell or Gibbon. Indeed, to seek after concreteness and effect would often prevent them from fulfilling their usual purpose—true knowledge and understanding of the contingent past. Modern history, for that matter, is not often guilty elite class which was the great achievement of eighteenth- and nineteenth-century civilization permitted and encouraged the historian or biographer to aim at both historical truth and literary force; the concerns of the scholar were not separate from the concerns of the human being. Now, of course, we have the often-lamented gap between the scholar and the journalist, between inert truth and cheap effect. The journalist, however, now seems pushed by the rising level of general culture towards adequacy to the human truth, and the scholar by the same phenomenon encouraged to discover that, though fact needs to be true to be valuable, it need not be dead in order to be true. Capote's book, Schlesinger's *Thousand Days*, Schorer's *Lewis* and Ellmann's *Joyce*, together with others that have recently appeared, may thus be harbingers of a renaissance in factual literature. We may hope so, for as Herbert Muller has shown, by precept and example, the past, of which materially we have recovered so much, must sometimes be put to immediately human uses if it is to serve us as fully as it may.

Boswell's Control of Aesthetic Distance

Paul K. Alkon

Proper control of aesthetic distance was so highly regarded by Johnson that he was sometimes inclined to undervalue biography. Thus in the *Idler*, No. 84, he argues that autobiography is more useful because "he that recounts the life of another, commonly dwells most upon conspicuous events, lessens the familiarity of his tale to increase its dignity, *shews his favourite at a distance* decorated and magnified like the ancient actors in their tragick dress, and endeavours to hide the man that he may produce a hero." Hence the failure of most biographers. They keep their heros too far away from us while, paradoxically, making them seem larger than life-size. Johnson's ideal for life-writing is clear: the less distance between reader and subject the better. Equally clear is Boswell's conscious adherence to that ideal.

Indeed Boswell's fame as an instigator of modern biography rests largely on his thorough rejection of the "doctrine of dignified distance." Using a variety of devices which are well recognized by critics, Boswell succeeded in bringing his readers close, often uncomfortably close, to Johnson. Early in the *Life of Johnson* and only four paragraphs after referring to the argument in the *Idler*, No. 84, Boswell explains his decision to let as little as possible, especially of the narrator, stand between readers and Johnson: "Instead of melting down my materials into one mass, and constantly speaking in my own person, by which I might have appeared to have more merit in the execution of the work, I . . . produce, wherever it is in my power, his own

From *University of Toronto Quarterly* 38, no. 2 (January 1969). Copyright © 1969 by University of Toronto Press.

minutes, letters, or conversation, being convinced that this mode is more lively." Neither Boswell nor his critics, however, have pointed out the crucial devices employed throughout the *Life* to increase and, in general, vary aesthetic distance in order to solve some of the literary problems confronting the biographer.

A major problem is hinted at by Boswell's equation of liveliness with "minutes, letters, or conversation." The reader's interest must somehow be sustained through a very long work. One method of doing so, Boswell implies, is to minimize distance by allowing his audience to remain in close touch with Johnson's own statements rather than with those statements seen at one remove through the filtering and perhaps distracting or tedious consciousness of an omnipresent narrator. Yet if Boswell faithfully kept to his promise of not *constantly* speaking in his own person, he was nevertheless uneasily aware of the fact that he did choose to remain what critics would now characterize as a highly intrusive, dramatized, self-conscious narrator-agent in his account of Johnson's life. Shortly before the conclusion, in somewhat ironic counterpoint to his initial statement of method, Boswell apologetically calls attention to his role as narrator: "I now relieve the readers of this Work from any farther personal notice of its authour, who if he should be thought to have obtruded himself too much upon their attention, requests them to consider the peculiar plan of his biographical undertaking."

Accepting this invitation to consider his "peculiar plan" does in fact lead to a better understanding of Boswell's artistic problems and his manipulation of aesthetic distance to cope with them. The peculiarity of his *Life* obviously does not consist in the mere presence of a narrator speaking in the first person to recount incidents and analyze character; nor is the chronological organization any novelty. What is distinctive, rather, is Boswell's announced effort to bring us close to Johnson by "interweaving what he privately wrote, and said, and thought; by which mankind are enabled as it were to see him live, and to 'live o'er each scene' with him." And the *Life*'s singularity is not only in taking readers strikingly close to Johnson's private self; perhaps an even more radical departure from traditional biography is Boswell's determination to present insofar as possible *each* scene—no matter how seemingly trivial—of Johnson's life. In principle, nothing was to be excluded. Everything recoverable was to be put on record. The work's peculiarity lies as much in its sheer quantity of close views as in their quality. This peculiarity too Boswell saw clearly and frequently explained apologetically. After describing how Johnson removed "branches of trees and other rubbish" from Taylor's waterfall, for example, Boswell adds: "This may be laughed at as too trifling to record; but it is a small characteristick trait in the Flemish picture which I give of my friend, and in which, therefore, I mark the most minute particulars." The scenes must not only focus on Johnson rather than on the potentially distracting narrator, but they must at their most trifling suggest what is characteristic of the subject.

Otherwise the *Life*, even when most closely attending to Johnson, will seem digressive. In the need to avoid this danger resides another major problem: that of creating and maintaining a coherent though necessarily complicated picture of Johnson to which all "minute particulars" will appear related. Without such coherency the biographical forest petrifies into dead wood. Corollary to this problem are the problems of maintaining faith in the reliability of the narrator and in the accuracy as well as the completeness of his "Flemish picture." Readers must be induced to trust the skill of a painter whose canvas is at once so large and so foreign to English practice. Moreover, as in all friendly biographies but especially in one whose peculiar plan entails unprecedentedly extensive close-up views, warts and all, there is the problem of maintaining the reader's love and respect for the subject. Finally, as the minute particulars pile up, through hundreds of pages, there is the problem of preventing readers kept this closely in Johnson's company from becoming so used to him that they forget what a remarkably *rara avis* Boswell is keeping in his biographical cage. Wayne Booth has correctly observed that "a prolonged intimate view of a character works against our capacity for judgment." Any judgment, he might have added, whether of merit or merely of singularity. There is thus considerable danger that our very familiarity with Johnson, induced by such close acquaintance with "what he privately wrote and said, and thought," may induce us to lose track of his astonishing uniqueness. Yet for the *Life* to succeed readers must at the conclusion still be able to feel the force of Hamilton's moving farewell to his friend: "He has made a chasm, which not only nothing can fill up, but which nothing has a tendency to fill up.—Johnson is dead.—Let us go to the next best:— there is nobody;—no man can be said to put you in mind of Johnson."

II

Not all of Boswell's artistic problems in writing the *Life* were dealt with entirely or even partly through control of aesthetic distance, to be sure. Most notably, his success in maintaining a coherent image of Johnson's character as a unifying principle of the *Life* was achieved by other means and therefore lies outside the scope of my discussion. Nor are the remaining problems I have listed resolved equally through the device of varying aesthetic distance. Boswell resorts most conspicuously to this technique, for example, in his effort to sustain interest in one man throughout a book which, though it cannot hope to compare in variety, rivals in bulk such works as Hume's *History of Great Britain*. If we tire of Alfred there is always William. If the feudal period bores us there is always the Elizabethan age. But what if the reader wearies of Johnson half-way through?

Since Boswell's professed and peculiar goal is to make readers "live o'er each *scene*" with Johnson, the *Life* is committed to the methods of drama. And to describe a performance as "dramatic" was then as it still is a way of saying that it is interesting. Going beyond the metaphor, however, critics are now in agreement on how, in general, the *Life* succeeds in aspiring to the condition of drama. There are stage directions: "Johnson (smiling), Sir. . . ." There is dialogue. There are even some conspicuous episodes such as the Wilkes dinner which are given the beginning-middle-and-end structure of a well-constructed play. In many of the more dramatic episodes, moreover, Boswell as narrator-dramatist is appropriately out of sight behind the scenes: having set the stage, he minimizes the distance between audience and events by cutting down references to himself ("I kept myself snug and silent") so that attention is focused on the other actors surrounding his hero. And because the essence of drama is talk, it is tempting to add to our growing list of critical commonplaces about Boswell's dramatic technique the fact that his commitment to dramatic method dictated a simple principle of decorum by which relevancy could be separated from tedious digression: commenting on his decision to exclude some "pleasant conversation" that Johnson had one day enjoyed hearing but in which he had not taken part, Boswell asserts that Johnson's "conversation alone, or what led to it, or was interwoven with it, is the business of this work."

But this plausible-sounding assertion will hardly do as an accurate or sufficient account of Boswell's method even at its most dramatic. In fact, the *Life*'s ability to sustain interest is due largely to Boswell's willingness to violate every aspect of the principle of decorum he so sweepingly enunciates here. He often includes material that is not part of Johnson's conversation or his life, that did not occasion Johnson's remarks, and that was in no direct sense "interwoven" with them. But this is not to say that such material is unrelated to Boswell's subject. Rather, it is to suggest that the relationship is far different from that which Boswell claims in his explicit statement of what may properly find a place in his book. That remark more accurately describes the effect than the methods of his artistry: where the

Life is successfully dramatic we are often only made to feel that Boswell has given us exclusively Johnson's talk, its causes, and what *"was"*—at the time the scene took place—"interwoven" with it. Sometimes we are indeed given these things. Often, however, the feeling is dramatic illusion. We have been induced to willing suspension of distinctions between past and present, as well as to suspension of our awareness of the difference between action on-stage and action off-stage.

Consider, for example, the following paragraph, complete in itself, and taken from a part of the record for 1776 where Boswell says that "to avoid a tedious minuteness" he will "group together what I have preserved of his conversation during this period . . . without specifying each scene where it passed" since "where the place or the persons do not contribute to the zest of the conversation, it is unnecessary to encumber my page with mentioning them." The dramatic method has been modified to the extent of dropping stage directions and the list of dramatis personae involved, but only in order—Boswell claims—to render the conversation, still his professed subject, as vigorously as possible:

> "There is much talk of the misery which we cause to the brute creation; but they are recompensed by existence. If they were not useful to man, and therefore protected by him, they would not be nearly so numerous." This argument is to be found in the able and benignant Hutchinson's 'Moral Philosophy.' But the question is, whether the animals who endure such sufferings of various kinds, for the service and entertainment of man, would accept of existence upon the terms on which they have it. Madam Sevigne, who, though she had many enjoyments, felt with delicate sensibility the prevalance of misery, complains of the task of existence having been imposed upon her without her consent.

What Johnson actually said occupies only the first two sentences, less than half of the passage. His opinion is followed by the seemingly digressive and gratuitous information that Johnson's opinion was also held by the Scot, Hutcheson. Conspicuously omitted is any claim that Johnson was influenced by *Moral Philosophy*. Indeed so far as Boswell knew, or at least so far as he reports in the *Life*, Johnson had not even read Hutcheson's book. Instead of urging any relationship other than coincidence of opinion between the two moralists, Boswell chooses to praise *Hutcheson's* ability and benevolence. Boswell as narrator then moves to the front of the stage where he proceeds in the next sentence to soliloquize on what the question is: whether animals would choose to be—that is the question. Finally, the passage moves far away from Johnson, his time, and his island to what was written on the continent in the preceding century by a French lady. One may properly ask whether Boswell has in constructing his paragraph contributed "to the zest of the conversation" or whether he has drifted away from conversation altogether and, like an unscrupulous performer, simply upstaged the great star. Is Boswell's dramatic method sometimes that of the ham actor?

Not in this case, certainly, for despite our initial doubts, it is clear that everything Boswell has done here conspires to produce the illusion—*effect* is a better term—of a lively, interesting, four way dialogue between Johnson, Hutcheson, Boswell, and Madame de Sévigné. That the dialogue not only never took place, but that it never could have since two of the "speakers" were dead in 1776, only reminds us that Boswell's imagination was not turned off by his determination to remain faithful to the truth, to *invent* nothing. There are other effects, too: finding him in agreement with the praiseworthy author of *Moral Philosophy* should raise or maintain our esteem for Johnson. Boswell, by his willingness to praise the moral and intellectual qualities of Hutcheson even while going on to indicate a deficiency in his (and Johnson's) statement of the question has minimized the moral distance between the narrator, Hutcheson, and Johnson: all are worthy men who can respect one another without falling into dull identity of viewpoint on an issue. By the same token, moral distance between Hutcheson, Johnson, and the reader is minimized. Identifying with the biographer in the absence of any reason here for feeling unlike him, the reader will adopt the narrator's moral kinship with men who are explicitly singled out for praise or implicitly praised by association. Madame de Sévigné, too, is made to seem morally close to all concerned: Boswell carefully characterizes her as a person who "felt with delicate sensibility the prevalence of misery." Along one axis, therefore, aesthetic distance has been sharply reduced.

Along another axis, however, distance is simultaneously increased. As the passage moves from Johnson's sentences to the viewpoints of Hutcheson, Boswell and Madam de Sévigné, the reader is taken further away intellectually from Johnson. His statement of the question is said to be inadequate, the topic is broadened from the misery of animals to the misery of people, and the lady is allowed to have the last word. There is no crushing retort from Johnson—"Madame (frowning)"—to bring readers back under the sway of his position and settle the matter. Nor does Boswell settle it. We are left only with the implication created by his restatement of the question, i.e., that Madame de Sévigné is more nearly right than Johnson.

But it is *we* who must finally decide. Boswell has in effect collapsed the distinction between actor and audience, between action onstage and action offstage. His drama—here as elsewhere throughout the *Life* primarily a play of ideas—becomes supremely interesting because he has put into it the most interesting of all possible characters: ourselves. It is a strikingly "modern" piece of dramaturgy. But as Professor Pottle has acutely pointed out, the current popularity of Boswell's journals is no accident due simply to their spicy night-scenes: "Boswell writes like one of us. His style raises few feelings of strangeness in the minds of readers whose taste has been fixed by Maugham, Hemingway, Joyce, Faulkner, Salinger." We are at home with Boswell's style for many reasons, but partly because he can so adroitly manipulate different aspects of aesthetic distance, as in the passage under discussion, to implicate us in his drama by keeping us morally (or emotionally) close to his cast of characters while nevertheless compelling us to stand back intellectually and pass judgment on the argument. Such manipulation does not occur in every scene of the *Life* any more than eloquent soliloquies occur in every act of Shakespeare's plays, but the occurrence is sufficiently frequent to warrant notice as a striking felicity of style. Of course one could read the Ten Commandments and then disagree with them. Any reader is always free to dispute any point. But some works do not *encourage* dissent as Boswell does in passages similar to the one I am discussing. His very deftness in sustaining interest by involving readers in the Johnsonian dialectic accounts for the dearth of critical comment on this aspect of his style. His art elegantly conceals itself, for it is only rarely that he makes his invitation as crudely explicit as for example he does when after describing one heated argument he says: "My readers will decide upon this dispute."

Even that comparatively crude invitation, however, serves to make the reader move away intellectually from Johnson, who otherwise would have had the last word in that argument when he silenced Boswell by growling "Nay, if you are to bring in gabble, I'll talk no more. I will not, upon my honour." In many scenes Boswell relies on another device for implicating readers and simulating conversation at that point in the narration where it is made clear that everyone has been reduced to silence by Johnson, all real conversation thereby ceasing. Consider, for example, the evening in 1775 at Cambridge's villa when Johnson, after giving his views on the harmlessness of *The Beggar's Opera*, brought the discussion to an abrupt halt by "collecting himself, as it were, to give a heavy stroke," and saying "There is in it such a *labefactation* of all principles, as may be injurious to morality." Johnson's remark is followed by two paragraphs, the second giving information on the stage history of *The Beggar's Opera* and the first providing the following information:

> While he pronounced this response, we sat in a comical sort of restraint, smothering a laugh, which we were afraid might burst out. In his Life of Gay, he has been still more decisive as to the inefficiency of 'The Beggar's Opera' in corrupting society. But I have ever thought somewhat differently; for, indeed, not only are the gaiety and heroism of a highwayman very captivating to a youthful imagination, but the arguments for adventurous depredation are so plausible, the allusions so lively, and the contrasts with the ordinary and more painful modes of acquiring property are so artfully displayed, that it requires a cool and strong judgement to resist so imposing an aggregate: yet, I own, I should be very sorry to have 'The Beggar's Opera' suppressed; for there is in it so much of real London life, so much brilliant wit, and such a variety of airs, which, from early association of ideas, engage, soothe, and enliven the mind, that no performance which the theatre exhibits, delights me more.

Here only the first two sentences are obviously relevant inasmuch as they finish describing the scene and then relate Johnson's conversation to his writing. Moreover, the first sentence increases our emotional distance from Johnson by showing that even the other actors in the scene found his remark funny. As the butt of ridicule, even silent ridicule, he is moved away from us. This comic distancing also reminds us of Johnson's uniqueness, for who but he could ever silence intelligent men by referring to labefactation?

The rest of the paragraph moves us away from Johnson intellectually as Boswell now occupies the stage alone, again soliloquizing: "I have ever thought somewhat differently. . . ." Though the effect is of discussion continued through more pros and cons (since Boswell proceeds to tell us what he has always thought on both sides of the issue), in fact the description of the scene has ended. We are not even given what Boswell thought *at the time* but was perhaps too intimidated to speak aloud; instead we merely have his lifelong ambivalent response to *The Beggar's Opera*. The question is, or is intended to be, complicated by Boswell's ruminations, and the reader is thereby presented with a dialectic whereas in fact during the scene described—that evening's conversation at Cambridge's villa—there was only a comical *ipse dixit*.

Boswell has deftly added to the comic interlude an intellectual pleasure.

After laughing, the reader must think about whose argument is most convincing. Very often more serious moments are also protracted in the same manner to make readers disengage themselves from Johnson's dicta and assess them. Having reported a conversation during which Johnson gave his views on marital infidelity, for example, Boswell adds a paragraph of disagreement beginning "Here it may be questioned, whether Johnson was entirely in the right." It is we who are left to settle the question. Again, after reporting Johnson's dismissal of *Elfrida* with the concession that it contains "now and then some good imitations of Milton's bad manner," Boswell registers dissent in a paragraph beginning "I often wondered at his low estimation of the writings of Gray and Mason." Having reported Johnson's refusal to concede that the "question concerning the legality of general warrants" was important, Boswell attributes the refusal to Johnson's characteristic "laxity of talking" and then adds that "surely, while the power of granting general warrants was supposed to be legal . . . we did not possess that security of freedom, congenial to our happy constitution, and which, by the intrepid exertions of Mr. Wilkes, has been happily established." By casting his opposition to Johnson in the form of praise for Wilkes, Boswell wrenches us intellectual miles if not light-years away from Johnson. We are of course always free to return. But simply by adding a sentence, Boswell has insured that agreement with Johnson on this issue will not be easy or thoughtless. Any siding with Johnson here that is not mere bias will only occur after the reader has mentally thrashed through the complicated question of Wilkes and liberty.

The list of similar examples could easily be lengthened. More significant than their mere presence as devices for engaging readers as "participants" in the Johnsonian intellectual drama, however, is the high degree of success Boswell has achieved. It has always been difficult for critics to remain indifferent to his Johnson. It is Boswell's skill as much as Johnson's personality that has created so many partisans and so many detractors. Even those who in Macaulay's vein disparage Boswell are in their way testifying to his effectiveness in forcing commitment, because it has usually been impossible merely to register dislike of the biographer without also inclining to preference for his subject. Even in a recent, sympathetic, and utterly unMacaulaian account of "the self-portrait of James Boswell which emerges from the conversations, letters, and editorial comments of the *Life of Johnson*," Irma S. Lustig was moved to deplore Boswell's "arrogant posthumous refutations of Johnson's views" on slavery. The corollary of her reaction is increased respect for the victim of Boswell's arrogance. And whatever in this fashion sustains or creates admiration for Johnson works towards an important goal of the *Life*. Boswell has created a rhetorical dilemma from which it is hard if not impossible to escape: agree with him and your opinion of Johnson, always finally admired by Boswell, goes up; disagree with or dislike him, and Johnson, by contrast, looks good.

Without so many Boswellian intrusions after the fact, the dilemma could not be posed in such acute form. Nor could it always function so effectively without Boswell's adroit blurring of the distinctions between past and present and between thought and word. In the above examples it has mostly been clear that Boswell is dissenting from Johnson at a safe distance in time: narrator and reader move away from the reported scene to its recollection in tranquillity. "*Here* it may be questioned whether Johnson was entirely in the right." Here in the book and now that he is gone. But not then and there. Often, however, the line between past and present is not so sharply drawn. After quoting Johnson's opinion of Rousseau, for example, Boswell has the last word by adding: "This violence seemed very strange to me, who had read many of Rousseau's animated writings with great pleasure, and even edification; had been much pleased with his society, and was just come from the Continent, where he was very generally admired. Nor can I yet allow that he deserves the very severe censure which Johnson pronounced upon him." In this case Boswell carefully distinguishes between his present opinion as he writes the biography and what he thought when he heard Johnson censure Rousseau. Yet the effect of so closely juxtaposing two consistently dissenting Boswellian opinions is to collapse the temporal distance between then and now. What seemed strange at the time still does. Nothing has shaken Boswell's admiration of Rousseau, which therefore gains at least some weight in our mental scales as it is balanced against Johnson's view. By the same juxtaposition, written word (what Boswell cannot yet allow as he writes the biography) coalesces with thought (what Boswell thought then about the strangeness of Johnson's violence). Similarly, Boswell's reported thought has for readers almost the same effect as disagreement spoken aloud. We see two sides of a "dialogue" whereas a witness of the scene itself (or a tape recording) would have noted only Johnson's remark and Boswell's silence.

Elsewhere Boswell more thoroughly collapses the distance between past and present. After quoting verbatim, for example, Johnson's remarks on Churchill's poetry—remarks incited, Boswell vaguely reports, by his having "ventured to hint that [Johnson] was not quite a fair judge"—the biographer adds: "In this depreciation of Churchill's poetry I could not agree with him.

It is very true that the greatest part of it is upon the topicks of the day. . . . But Churchill had extraordinary vigour. . . . Let me add, that there are in his works many passages which . . ." The paragraph from which these extracts are taken moves smoothly from past ("I could not agree") to present tense ("it is very true. . . . Let me add") via a listing of the attributes of Churchill's poetry. Most often any such list will be in the present tense, whether or not it is part of a reported thought or statement that occurred in the past. With such a passage serving as bridge, readers are less aware of the switch in tense. Moreover there is some ambiguity about Boswell's statement that he "could not agree" with Johnson. Does this mean that Boswell was silent? Or does it mean that he spoke aloud arguments like— but not verbally identical with—those that he gives in the paragraph?

These questions are significant precisely because they do not occur to most readers of the *Life*. So deftly has Boswell collapsed the distance between past and present in this and similar passages that we are normally aware only of the effect he thereby creates: dialogue is imitated with elegant artifice. Here, as in other ways elsewhere, Boswell's art achieves its success not by transcription of life but rather by skilful mimesis.

III

Most often temporal distance is minimized without conspicuously lessening intellectual distance between readers and Johnson. Especially is this the case in the many extreme instances where Boswell simply takes his readers completely back into the past by omitting any explicit reference to the act or moment of writing, giving instead merely what Johnson said together with what Boswell was moved to *think* in response. A few examples will suffice: "Here he seemed to me to be strangely deficient in taste; for surely statuary is a noble art of imitation. . . ."; "My illustrious friend, I thought, did not sufficiently admire Shenstone. . . ."; "I, however, could not help thinking that a man's humour is often uncontroulable by his will" "Seeing him heated, I would not argue any farther; but I was confident that I was in the right. I would, in due time, be a Nestor, an elder of the people; and there *should* be some difference between the conversation of twenty-eight and sixty-eight." In noting these and similar passages where Boswell's dissent maintains significant intellectual distance between readers and Johnson, however, it must be remembered that such distance is always a comparatively short remove from Johnson and from the narrator's reiterated position of affinity to his "illustrious friend." It is somewhat surprising to discover how often Boswell actually disagrees with Johnson, because what the narrator causes to stand out most prominently in our memories of the *Life* are the places where he describes his response to Johnson in such phrases as "I thought I could defend him at the point of my sword. My reverence and affection for him were in full glow."

Historically, most readers have been left with an overwhelming impression of Boswell standing close to Johnson in rapt attention and enthusiastic accord. Boswell's kinship with the master has so far exceeded that of all but the most sympathetic readers as to become proverbial: only recently has *Webster's New International Dictionary* stopped defining *Boswellian* as "Relating to, or characteristic of Dr. Johnson's biographer, James Boswell, whose hero worship made a faithful but often uncritical record of details." But this impression, like the reader's memory of almost unceasing dialogue, is partly dramatic illusion. Boswell has in fact chosen to remain in the middle distance between objective spectator and hero-worshipper. He portrays himself as sufficiently close to the average reader so that the narrator functions as Everyman reacting to the unique Johnson while nevertheless remaining close enough to the Sage in outlook and disposition so that readers will accept the biographer as a fit guide.

Upon the success of Boswell's difficult balancing act depends much of the effectiveness of "the peculiar plan of his biographical undertaking." Imagine for a moment a *Life of Johnson* written in the grand manner of, say, Winston Churchill, Gibbon, or even of Johnson himself. Imagine that all the Johnsonian dialogue is retained together with the distinctive piling up of "each scene" of which there is some record. But suppose that for Boswell's personality *as it is revealed to us in his book* the personality of Gibbon, or Churchill, or some twin of Johnson were substituted. There is no reason why such a *Life* could not be successful. But it would be a radically different kind of success. We as readers would be kept at a greater distance from the subject by the imposing personality of the narrator. There would always be the distancing realization, as there is for example in reading Johnson's lives of the greater poets, that we are watching from a respectful distance one extraordinary mind respond to another. The spectacle may be fascinating, but we cannot become part of it in the way Boswell makes us participants in the drama of Johson's life, living "o'er each scene *with* him."

To maintain the narrator equidistant from readers and Johnson, Boswell plays many roles throughout the *Life*. Extremes are intended to cancel each other out. Sometimes he is simply like his presumed readers, the literate Everyman intelligently in touch with the current state of *belles lettres*. Thus, early in the *Life*, commenting on the publication of *London*, he remarks: "To us who have long known the manly force, bold spirit, and masterly versification of this poem, it is a matter of curiosity to observe the diffidence with which its author brought it forward into publick notice." Here by his choice of plural pronoun Boswell joins the group of readers long familiar with one of the century's most famous poems. Distance between narrator and audience is collapsed to the point of complete identification. He becomes one of us. Much later in the *Life* Boswell quotes a passage of self-analysis written in his journal *after* an evening with Johnson, asserting in defense of the quotation: "This reflection, which I thus freely communicate, will be valued by the thinking part of my readers, who may have themselves experienced a similar state of mind." Together with its attempt to disarm through bullying and flattery any charge of irrelevancy, this sentence endeavors to move narrator and reader close together intellectually by suggesting a probable kinship of mental experience. Boswell thus reassures his intelligent readers that he is like them.

He usually does so less explicitly by disclosing the narrator's character in ways that invite readers to infer their likeness to him. After quoting, for example, Johnson's statement that the most famous men worry most about losing their reputation, Boswell adds: "I silently asked myself, 'Is it possible that the great SAMUEL JOHNSON really entertains any such apprehension, and is not confident that his exalted fame is established upon a foundation never to be shaken?'" Here the narrator portrays himself as an ordinary, unfamous man startled to catch a close glimpse of the uncertainties of greatness. Readers not suffering delusions of grandeur will by this sentence and similar ones be moved closer to the narrator and thereby encouraged to continue their identification with him, seeing Johnson through eyes that might—so Boswell makes us feel—belong to any man.

To ensure, however, that such identification by readers with the narrator does not become so close that confidence in him as fit guide is rattled by any feeling that he is *just* an ordinary man, no different from the run-of-the-mill reader of biographies, Boswell frequently invites attention to his own distinctiveness. At no point in the *Life* are we allowed to forget that the narrator, unlike his readers, was after all one of the charmed circle admitted to friendship with "the great SAMUEL JOHNSON." Nor does Boswell omit to remind us, albeit with disarming wit, of how the members of Johnson's circle differ from the rest of us: "Dr. Goldsmith, being a privileged man, went with him this night, strutting away, and calling to me with an air of superiority, like that of an esoterick over an exoterick disciple of a sage of antiquity, 'I go to Miss Williams.' I confess, I then envied him this mighty privilege, of which he seemed so proud; but it was not long before I obtained the same mark of distinction."

Not that all members of Johnson's circle are to be equally respected. Boswell's reiterated sniping at Hawkins and Mrs. Thrale is only part of a sustained effort intended to display the narrator as remarkable both for his illustrious friendships and for his unusually selfless devotion to the exacting task of accurately portraying Johnson. After briefly marvelling at his own talents, Boswell says in the Advertisement to the first edition that he "will only observe, as a specimen of my trouble, that I have sometimes been obliged to run half over London, in order to fix a date correctly; which, when I had accomplished, I well knew would obtain me no praise, though a failure would have been to my discredit." Elsewhere in the *Life* Boswell's painstaking humility is brought to our attention. No seeker after praise, the narrator is only "desirous that my work should be, as much as is consistent with the strictest truth, an antidote to the false and injurious notions of his character, which have been given by others." Though "others" have been slanderous, Boswell is simply the *vir bonus* motivated in all matters by "my earnest love of truth." But his humility does not of course exclude selfless literary courage in a worthy cause: "To please the true, candid, warm admirers of Johnson, and in any degree increase the splendour of his reputation, I bid defiance to the shafts of ridicule, or even of malignity." Brave Boswell! It is not everyone—certainly not every reader, however well disposed to Johnson—who would feel equally willing to expose himself for the cause. As in these and other similar statements Boswell displays his moral and intellectual fitness for his biographical task he is also precluding the possibility of excessive identification by readers with the narrator. Though similar, they are not to be thought identical. He has written the book. They have not. At the outset Boswell calls attention to this elementary though crucial distinction by asserting: "The labour and anxious attention with which I have collected and arranged the materials of which these volumes are composed, will hardly be conceived by those who read them with careless facility." Readers speeding through the *Life* are thus reminded of their distance from its author. So far are they from him intellectually that his immense labors will be almost beyond their ken.

Another way of avoiding over-familiarity with readers is to put on the mask of Johnsonian sage, however ill-fitting. Boswell moves away from us— in the direction of Johnson—by assuming that we need advice and then supplying it. "The excellent Mr. Nelson's 'Festivals and Fasts' . . . is a most valuable help to devotion; and in addition to it I would recommend two sermons on the same subject, by Mr. Pott, Archdeacon of St. Alban's, equally distinguished for piety and elegance." Here readers are reduced to students taking their reading list from the pious, learned narrator. After mastering Pott's sermons, the open-minded reader may wish advice on whether to support abolitionists: "I have read, conversed, and thought much upon the subject, and would recommend to all who are capable of conviction, an excellent Tract by my learned and ingenious friend John Ranby, Esq. entitled 'Doubts on the Abolition of the Slave Trade.'" Does the reader perhaps have children? "No book whatever can be recommended to young persons, with better hopes of seasoning their minds with *vital religion*, than YOUNG'S 'NIGHT THOUGHTS.'" Of the importance of treating an errant daughter sternly Boswell leaves the possibly wavering reader in no doubt: "After frequently considering this subject, I am more and more confirmed in what I then meant to express, and which was sanctioned by the authority and illustrated by the wisdom of Johnson; and I think it of the utmost consequence to the happiness of Society, to which subordination is absolutely necessary. It is weak, and contemptible, and unworthy, in a parent to relax in such a case." Boswell goes on, but this much sufficiently illustrates one of his more vehement moves in the direction of the firm-minded Johnsonian sage, agreeing with the master in something like the master's magisterial tone.

Boswell also affects the Johnsonian tone by sententiously generalizing on the human condition: "To such unhappy chances are human friendships liable. . . ." Or, for another example, after stating his disagreement with the philosophy of *Rasselas* and then affirming that life is sometimes more, and sometimes less happy, Boswell launches another flight of somber religious advice by saying: "This I have learnt from a pretty hard course of experience, and would, from sincere benevolence, impress upon all who honour this book with a perusal, that until a steady conviction is obtained that the present life is an imperfect state, and only a passage to a better. . . ." Nothing better illustrates the mask Boswell is trying to wear in such passages than his soliloquy on "how different a place London is to different people." Placing himself momentarily in their shoes, the narrator concisely describes how the city will seem to "a politician . . . a grazier . . . a mercantile man . . . a dramatick enthusiast . . . a man of pleasure" and, finally, to such men as the narrator himself: "But the intellectual man is struck with it, as comprehending the whole of human life in all its variety, the contemplation of which is inexhaustible." Throughout the *Life* Boswell tries to portray himself as an intellectual man, just as throughout the *London Journal* he tries equally hard to cast himself in a very different role: "The description is faint;

but I surely may be styled a Man of Pleasure. . . . I patrolled up and down Fleet Street, thinking on London, the seat of Parliament and the seat of pleasure, and seeming to myself as one of the wits in King Charles the Second's time."

Equally illustrative of the role Boswell adopts in his *London Journal*—and of the fact that he does conspicuously put on different masks to match different rhetorical situations in different books—is the moment when he reports that he "drank about and sung *Youth's the Season* and thought myself Captain Macheath." In the *Life* our narrator does not try to persuade readers that he is a Restoration rake or a character in search of a comic opera. Instead there are the solemn warnings and sober generalizations together with a very different and much more respectable order of literary allusions. Thus after describing how he has educated his sons, Boswell adds his expectation that "they will, like Horace, be grateful to their father for giving them so valuable an education." We readers may well feel put back in our (distant) place by such glimpses of the generalizing Scottish sage as intellectual man in London or at home raising so wisely his Horatian family.

Or we may smile. And in that case Boswell's control of aesthetic distance has wavered. Instead of moving away from readers in the direction of Johnson, the narrator has moved away in the opposite direction, far alike from Johnson and from the readers to whom the narrator has become an object of ridicule. Consider, for example—everyone will have his own favorite—Boswell at grips with the problem of getting up in the morning: "I have thought of a pulley to raise me gradually; but that would give me pain, as it would counteract my internal inclination." Here the would-be intellectual man looks suspiciously like Falstaff. Too often throughout the *Life* Boswell comes onstage wearing the wrong mask.

Control of aesthetic distance has not wavered every time we smile at the narrator, however. After one memorable Johnsonian retort, for example, Boswell interrupts his narrative by observing: "I never heard the word *blockhead* applied to a woman before, though I do not see why it should not, when there is evident occasion for it." Here readers may well laugh at Boswell's naïvely solemn consideration of the great lexicographer's word usage. But the narrator has conspicuously placed tongue in cheek to heighten our appreciation of a comic incident. While pausing to smile at the narrator readers must also stand apart from what Johnson has just said and reflect on how extraordinary the remark really was. It is only when our laughter at Boswell deflects attention from Johnson that control of aesthetic distance has been lost. All readers would not agree on precisely where and how often these mistakes occur. Nor is it necessary to achieve such accord. The acceptance for so long of Macaulay's response to Boswell is sufficient evidence of the *Life*'s most conspicuous flaw; Boswell's characterization of the narrator does not always keep readers at a respectful distance which is nevertheless sufficiently close to him for that identification which induces maximum involvement in the *Life*'s play of ideas. Where the *Life* fails it is because we are allowed to come too close to the narrator or, what is in effect perhaps the same thing, because he is pushed too far away from us in the wrong direction.

But to pinpoint the *Life*'s weak spot as a wavering in control of aesthetic distance between readers and narrator is not to say that the weakness is fatal. Boswell's overwhelming achievement in creating the most famous biography in the English language is in large though not exclusive measure due to his skill in varying different aspects of aesthetic distance. The places where his control falters are comparatively few and, because he does succeed in establishing the rhetorical dilemma which I have described above, even those places do not significantly undercut the *Life*'s over-all effect. The brief examples discused here typify the ways in which by varying aesthetic distance along several axes Boswell succeeds in sustaining interest, maintaining faith in the narrator, creating sympathy for Johnson, and, perhaps most important of all, preventing the reader's sensibilities from being anesthetized by such thorough immersion in the "Johnsonian aether" as Boswell's peculiar plan entails. By compelling us so often to stand back and weigh Johnson's distinctive remarks, by thus reminding us of how debatable his views so often are, Boswell keeps alive our sense of wonder. We are never allowed to forget that Samuel Johnson was "a man whose talents, acquirements, and virtues were so *extraordinary*, that the more his character is considered the more he will be regarded by the present age, and by posterity, with admiration and reverence."

The *Life of Johnson*:
Art and Authenticity

Frederick A. Pottle

"What I consider as the peculiar value of the following work," wrote Boswell in the paragraphs introductory to the *Life of Johnson*, "is the quantity that it contains of Johnson's conversation." The emphasis is on the word "peculiar," and in what follows I shall retain that emphasis. Boswell's strategies as a biographer, his handling of conversation apart, are impressive and worthy of analysis, but they are not strikingly different from those employed by other biographers. His conversations, by general consent, are unique, and they do constitute the supreme value of his work.

Study of Boswell's journal in the forty years or so since its recovery has added nothing to the value of the *Life* as a work of art, but it has revolutionized our thinking about the way in which the book was written and the nature of Boswell's genius. Gone forever is the assumption that he subordinated the claims of his own life to the recording of Johnson's; gone is the picture of him trotting at Johnson's elbow with a notebook, anxiously jotting down Johnson's conversation for use in a biography. We know now that he was an inordinately ambitious man who lived his own life fully; we know that with only trifling exceptions he recorded the conversations in his journal, sometimes long after they occurred. And we know that he put the conversations in the journal primarily because they were a most important part of his own life.

Boswell was remarkable for his zest in life and his consciousness of enjoyment. The first of these traits is common, the second rare. And he added to these a third trait so uncommon as to appear unique. He did not feel that his zest had been exhausted, his enjoyment fully enjoyed, till he had made a lively *written* record of it, till he had journalized it. "I should live no more than I can record," he wrote, "as one should not have more corn growing than one can get in." He was in London when he made that observation, but the context makes clear that Johnson's conversation was only the contribution of his best field to the bumper crop he was having difficulty in getting under cover. As Geoffrey Scott has said, the Johnsonian portions of Boswell's journal are not different in kind from the rest; they flow in and out with no change whatever in method or emphasis. "The vast, bracing difference is the subject matter."

Boswell's compulsion to record his own life is to my knowledge unique for urgency and sharpness of definition, but one does not have to look far for an illuminating parallel. If a man wrote, "I should construct no more plots than I can write down," we should know at once that we had to do with a practicing author, and probably with a successful one. Well, Boswell felt in the day-by-day happenings of his own mind the overriding significance which novelists feel in their inchoate fictions; and he felt the same pressure that they do to bring *his* matter to full literary expression. *Literary* (or, if you prefer, *imaginative*) expression is important, for we must not suppose that Boswell's recurring stretches of terse, dry chronicle or of abbreviated and cryptic notes were felt by him to be anything more than ground-holding operations. Gone with the obsequious Boswell and the notebook Boswell is the amateur Boswell, the Boswell who embarked on serious writing at the age of forty-five. The journal from its earliest period shows the alert awareness of literary problems that marks a gifted and practiced writer. "I observe continually," he wrote at the age of twenty-nine, "how imperfectly upon most occasions words preserve our ideas. . . . In description we omit insensibly many little touches that give life to objects. With how small a speck does a painter give life to an eye!" Boswell not only had literary imagination to a high degree, but his imagination worked specifically and continually in literary recording of the daily matter of his own experience, including Johnson. It made an incalculable difference to the quality of the *Life* that he did not merely store notes and wait till he was middle-aged before he attempted the full imaginative expression of the conversations which were to shape and to dominate his book. Thanks to his journalizing, he had begun applying his best literary powers to Johnson at the age of twenty-two, with twenty-two years left in which to test and improve his method.

"Little touches that give life to objects"—one finds no language of this kind in the "Advertisements" to the *Life* or in the introductory paragraphs in which Boswell discusses his method. He firmly claims credit for "labour and anxious attention" in collecting and arranging his materials, for "stretch of mind and prompt assiduity" in preserving conversations, and for the "degree of trouble" he had put himself to to "ascertain with a scrupulous authenticity" the "innumerable detached particulars" of which his book consists. Nothing more. I suppose even a vainer author might hesitate to proclaim his artistry in advance of the verdict of the public, but I suspect another motive for silence. He was determined above all things that readers should not only grant his claim of scrupulous authenticity in the detached particulars, but should also assume an equal degree of authenticity in his overall depiction of Johnson; and he may have feared that any talk about his *giving* life to objects would imply that he had colored fact with fiction. Whatever the motive, he gives, and seems to have intended to give, the impression that all that was needed to produce the *Life* was a remarkable memory and lots of hard work. It is this impression, no less erroneous for having been initiated by Boswell himself, that I now wish to demolish.

Boswell, by birth or self-training or both, did have a remarkable memory. Furnished with the right kind of clue and given time, patience, and freedom from distraction, he could bring back any desired portion of his past with a wealth of authentic detail; particularly, could recover a good part of what he and other people had really said on that occasion. The right kind of clue was a written note made by himself; nothing else would serve. Without such a note, his memory was no better than anyone else's. I think he would have preferred to post his journal soon enough after the events so that no note would have been necessary, but there were few periods in his life when he could journalize with that degree of regularity. His more general practice was to make rough, abbreviated notes on scraps of waste paper soon after the events, the sooner the better. From these he wrote up the journal days, months, even years later, as he could find time.

The notes often seem quite disorderly and unselective, as though Boswell, in a tearing hurry, were jotting down whatever rose first to consciousness. When he had expanded the notes in a journal, he almost invariably threw them away. This is of crucial importance in any discussion of his method. If he never got around to write the journal, he would cite the notes as authority, but he never assigned to notes an authority superior to that of the journal based on them. *Faute de mieux,* the notes were a record ("the bones," he himself said) of his life, but their primary and essential function was to serve as hints for remembering. ("A hint such as this brings to my mind all that passed, though it would be barren to anybody but myself.")

The process of recollection did not stop with the journal, but continued to operate when matter from the journal was transferred to the *Life*. The greater part of the extended Johnsonian conversations involving several speakers, it now appears, had never been expanded in the journal at all, and had to be worked up from notes jotted down many years before. One also frequently finds Boswell adding sentences and paragraphs to portions of fully written journal. Some of these additions seem to be authentic but undated recollections for which he had to find plausible points of attachment; others, I have no doubt, are a second crop of memory, gathered as he relived the matter he had copied.

Boswell's insistence on the essentiality of circumstantial detail in all recording of the past was probably in part due to his own need for a body of authentic and unique historical detail if he were to set his memory in successful operation. Circumstances were a bridgehead into the forgotten country; if he held the bridgehead, he could reoccupy the country at will. And reoccupation was an effort, was by no means automatic. It now appears probable that some—perhaps all—human brains do store specific physical traces of massive coherent quantities of past sense-experience, and that appropriate stimulus will cause a person to relive such clusters in minute detail, for example, will enable the stimulated person to listen in on an old conversation in its entirety, or hear an orchestra play through a piece of music just as he heard it years before. Boswell's memory was almost certainly not of that sort. So far as our present-day knowledge goes, that kind of recall requires physical stimulus of an abnormal sort—an adventitious current of electricity. Besides, Boswell's recall, as I hope to demonstrate, does not bear the marks of passive or rote memory. He seems rather to have been a champion in a game we all play at all the time; and his performance appears to be no less explicable in terms of genetic aptitude and sedulous training than the performance of any other champion. Many examples of equally extraordinary memory have been cited. William Lyon Phelps says that his older brother Dryden could remember some definite thing that had happened to him on every day of his life after the age of five. If you asked him, "What did you do on February 17, 1868?" he would ponder about twenty seconds and then say, "That was a Monday," and in about three minutes he would describe the weather on that day and tell you something he had done on it. The fixing of the day of the week which seemed so remarkable to Phelps was a simple arithmetical calculation which many people could perform in their heads if they knew the formula, but back of the recall of the events of the particular day undoubtedly lay extended special training of some sort. When I ask myself what could have been the groundwork for that training, I get a mental picture of a shelf full of little books—a long unbroken row of calendar diaries, begun at the age of five and kept without a single blank for more than sixty-five years. At any rate, Boswell's journal, with its subsidiary notes and memoranda, was not merely a record of the past; it was also persistent and scrupulous training in recollection.

Boswell never maintained that his records of conversation were complete word-for-word transcripts of what was said on a given occasion, though perhaps by silence he encouraged readers to think that they were. They are obviously epitomes or miniatures: people talking for the length of time he says or implies that they did talk would certainly have uttered many more words than appear in his account. If we had a tape-recording of the originals of any of the conversations in the *Life,* we should find that the progression of the dialogue was by no means as swift and economical as the *Life* represents it to have been. Real speakers in real life—even Johnson's— wander off in side-excursions and bog down in irrelevancies. The conversations of the *Life* are in this respect not unlike the brief reports of long extemporaneous speeches in Parliament that one finds in eighteenth- century newspapers and magazines. The reporter has condensed the speeches in language which he was not given verbatim but had to find for himself, yet he has infused the styles of the speakers into his condensations.

One can get a nice definition of Boswell's method by combining two remarks which he himself made. At the end of the first extended conversation he recorded in his journal—a conversation which he and his friend Andrew Erskine had with David Hume on 4 November 1762—he congratulated himself on having "preserved the heads and many of the words" of a dialogue lasting an hour and a half. His record comprises less than a thousand words. And he says (this time in the *Life of Johnson*) that when, in the course of time his mind became *"strongly impregnated with the Johnsonian aether,"* he could carry Johnson's remarks in his memory and commit them to paper "with much more facility and exactness." This answers a number of questions which have been put as to the historical veridicality of his Johnsonian record. Did Boswell ever follow Plato's practice, inventing for Johnson extended dialogues which were appropriate but non-historical? No. Boswell's Johnson is always "authentic": his Johnson speaks on the major topics ("heads") of conversations actually entered into by the historical Johnson. Did Boswell, while sticking to the historical "heads," ever allow himself to extend

Johnson's remarks by fictitious matter serving purposes of Boswell's own? No. Boswell's Johnson is in this respect "*scrupulously* authentic." He does not say *all* that the historical Johnson said on a given occasion, but he says nothing that the historical Johnson did not in substance say—on that occasion or another. For Boswell indeed admits in the journal (unfortunately not in the *Life*) that he does not always observe strict chronology in recording Johnson's remarks. These admissions, I believe, all occur in journals like the Hebridean journal of 1773 or the Ashbourne journal of 1777, on occasions when he was continuously in Johnson's company, had fallen behind in his effort to keep the journal up to the preceding day, and feared that he would lose some vivid recollection if he put off recording it till its proper date was reached. To me the fact that the admittedly displaced sayings fit their surroundings so perfectly suggests that an additional principle may have been operating, at least part of the time. In all conversation between intimate friends, the same topics keep recurring; and, when they do recur, most speakers repeat themselves almost automatically and almost verbatim. Johnson's "exuberant variety" generally protected him from flaccid repetition; and Boswell, when the same topic occurred twice in matter still unjournalized, may sometimes have conflated the two versions in the journal, using the portions of each which at the time he considered superior. Or, when he felt sure that he had already reported Johnson on a given topic, he may sometimes not have put the second version into the journal at all. The unrecorded variants, I suggest, hung in his memory as authentic Johnsoniana, and in the *Life* sometimes replaced or were added to the readings of the journal he had before him. This is admittedly speculation, but it is, I believe, the speculation likely to be advanced by anyone who has patiently worked through the vast body of documentation underlying the *Life*.

Does Boswell, then, report Johnson's conversation verbatim? In particular sentences and in some brief passages of an epigrammatic cast, yes. In general, no. The crucial words, the words that impart the peculiar Johnsonian quality, are indeed *ipsissima verba*. Impregnated with the Johnsonian ether, Boswell was able confidently to recall a considerable body of characteristic diction. Words entail sense; and when elements of the remembered diction were in balance or antithesis, recollection of words and sense would almost automatically give "authentic" sentence structure. But in the main Boswell counted on impregnation with the Johnsonian ether (that is, on an understanding, grown intuitive, of Johnson's habits of composition) to help him consciously to construct epitomizing sentences in which the *ipsissima verba* would be at home. His greatest virtue an an imitator or re-creator of Johnson's style was not to overdo the idiosyncrasies. Long stretches of his journal, recorded as indirect discourse, were converted into Johnsonian utterance with no more revision than a change of pronouns and tenses.

"With how small a speck does a painter give life to an eye!"—we are back to Boswell's dictum, better able, I hope, to consider its import after this excursus on his memory. Johnson's conversation as Boswell reported it, is, for all its veridicality, an imaginative reconstruction, a recreation; it is embedded in a narrative made continuously lively by unobtrusive specks of imagination. The stylistic unity of the *Life* has not been enough remarked on. The conversations in the *Life* melt into the narrative; one light of imagination pervades the whole. The Johnsonian ether, which I have just defined narrowly as "an understanding, grown intuitive, of Johnson's habits of composition," was, at a deeper level, a massively detailed conception of Johnson's character, operating to shape into unity all the multifarious and potentially discordant elements of a very long book.

A biographer who aims at this kind of unity (that is, who aims at literature) must win and keep control of his book. The view of the subject's character presented must be *his* view, not the subject's. There is no doubt that the eye that has seen Johnson in the *Life* is Boswell's, but at first glance it is a little hard to see how he managed to keep it so. In incorporating so many complete and largely unselected letters of Johnson, for example, he took a great chance, the chance that so much of Johnson's own strong and idiosyncratic style, so much of Johnson's own casual comment on casual happenings, would force open the focusing tension and reduce the book to a mere compilation. But Boswell counted on the conversations to dominate and control the letters, and he did not trust in vain. In the conversations, as we have seen, he remembered the heads and the very words of a great part of what Johnson had actually said on many occasions. But the heads had more often than not been proposed by himself and were of intense personal concern to himself, and the whole had been sifted by *his* memory and vitalized by *his* imagination. He had reconstructed the conversations in the first place to complete portions of his own life in which he had felt himself to be living most fully, and to savor that completeness. The conversations, though they appear to be pure Johnson, are in fact the quintessence of Boswell's view of Johnson.

Johnson's Johnson

Richard B. Schwartz

> *Nothing paints a truly great Man in Colours that strike the Eyes of the discerning Mind with more Energy, and captivating Force, than a Confession of his Weakness from his own Mouth.*
>
> —*Life of Boerhaave*

Boswell acknowledges the validity of Johnson's preference for autobiography over biography but justifies his own endeavors by pointing out that Johnson's autobiographical comments are scattered and fragmentary. Implicitly, the desultory labors of Johnson are contrasted with the assiduity of Boswell, the "persevering diligence" upon which Boswell prides himself and upon which he stakes his claims as biographer:

> Had Dr. Johnson written his own life, in conformity with the opinion which he has given, that every man's life may be best written by himself; had he employed in the preservation of his own history, that clearness of narration and elegance of language in which he has embalmed so many eminent persons, the world would probably have had the most perfect example of biography that was ever exhibited. But although he at different times, in a desultory manner, committed to writing many particulars of the progress of his mind and fortunes, he never had persevering diligence enough to form them into a regular composition. Of these materials a few have been preserved; but the greater part was consigned by him to the flames, a few days before his death.
>
> *(Life)*

From *Boswell's Johnson: A Preface to the "Life."* Copyright © 1978 by the Board of Regents of the University of Wisconsin System. University of Wisconsin Press, 1978.

We shall never know the precise nature of the materials which Johnson burned. Of the materials which remain, certain things may be said. The fragment which Johnson probably termed "Annals" was not seen by Boswell although it fully vindicates Boswell's judgment of the likely nature of an extended Johnsonian autobiography. It is, in its way, superior to anything in Boswell's *Life*. Its details are vivid, touching, and extremely suggestive. The fragment abounds in quotable passages (some involving dialogue) which provide striking insights into the nature of Johnson's family and his early life with them. It should be reread whenever one is on the verge of lavishing praise on Boswell, for it indicates what we might have had.

In a sense the practices which Johnson follows in his "Annals" conflict with an aspect of his biographical theory which Boswell utilizes. Much has been made of the cumulative pattern of Boswell's *Life*. Because Boswell assumes a relatively static notion of personality his task is to collect specimens of the various aspects of Johnson's personality. He is not obliged to weight his materials equally and he is not obliged to give equal attention to each year of Johnson's life. This notion of personality, child-as-father-of-man, justifies the structure of the *Life* and allows Boswell—with individual specimens or within individual scenes—to transcend temporal constraints and refer to earlier or later events or pronouncements. Moreover, as I just indicated, Boswell has Johnsonian precedent for this view of personality; he appropriately cites Johnson's *Life of Sydenham* in this regard. This view of personality conflicts with the well-known comments of Hume concerning the nature of identity. Hume, of course, argues that identity *per se* does not exist. There is no static identity to which we may point, for we inhabit a world of constant change and our identity is perforce the sum of all our experience at a particular moment. If one is to describe identity one must (as Johnson does in his "Annals") examine the stores of memory, for it is there that "identity" resides. In short, if one is to examine another's personality he must have a detailed sense of the experiences—and the associations attending them—of the biographical subject. Boswell's ignorance of this kind of information, particularly concerning Johnson's youth, severely limits his ability to understand Johnson's personality. I am not criticizing Boswell here, only pointing out the constraints within which he was forced to work.

The stores of memory represent somewhat intractable material even for the autobiographer for there is no way that he can present those materials to his reader in all of their fullness. This is part of the point of *Tristram Shandy*, of course. The autobiographer, like the biographer, is forced to shape his materials and present an image of the self, built of selected details though based on a knowledge of all details. Thus Hume's "My Own Life" is essentially a character, not an autobiography. Gibbon's *Memoirs* is an elaborate labor of self-love which involves highly conscious shaping and the most carefully considered utilization of phrase, detail, and scene.

It is useful, doubtless, to record experience in varied fashion so that the complexities of detail and the shaping of detail are apparent. Thus Johnson, for example, writes the "Annals" but also the *Prayers and Meditations,* which record responses to patterns of experience of a different order and—in their temporal dimension—of a different rhythm. Then too, there are passages suggesting the concerns of account books and appointment calendars as well as the detailed, clinical "Aegri Ephemeris." Boswell does this sort of thing himself, moving from notes to journal to literary text, from detailed jottings to finished characters and self-portraits. Some records are nearly clinical, some highly artificial and involving elaborate literary devices. But Johnson also indulged in self-portraiture and it is here that Boswell is open to criticism. Autobiographical passages abound in Johnson's works and, in my judgment, the self-portraits follow a discernible pattern, one of which Boswell is aware but one which he does not fully utilize. Boswell could not have access to *all* information on Johnson and it is both unrealistic and unfair to expect him to examine all *available* information, some of which it has taken centuries to fully recover. My concern is with Boswell's reluctance (or failure) to use materials which were readily available. If I am correct, the ultimate weakness of the *Life* is its lack of a coherent, sophisticated "image" of Johnson, an image based on all readily available details, an image which would enable Boswell to shape his materials in such a way as to present a reasonably reliable sense of the personality and character of his biographical subject. Within his own works Johnson provides such an image.

"Boswell's Johnson" is defended in strange ways. While acknowledging the fact that every portrait will be affected by subjective coloring—there is no image that is truly final—it is curious that Boswell's is defended on such grounds as longevity and popular acceptance. Johnson's Johnson, the Johnson nearly always forgotten in this type of discussion, is potentially of far greater importance than any of its competitors. It is not an elaborately detailed image but its simplicity is a crucial part of the conception itself. At any rate, it tells us much more than the fact that Johnson was both great and good.

The personal dimension of Johnson's works has not been overlooked. We know, for example, on Mrs. Piozzi's authority, that Johnson portrayed friends and acquaintances in his periodical essays *(Anecdotes)*. She also contends that "many of the severe reflections on domestic life in Rasselas, took their source from its author's keen recollections of the time passed in his early years," and that Johnson had his own mother in mind when he described peaceful old age in ll. 291-98 of *The Vanity of Human Wishes (Anecdotes)*. On John Nichols' authority, Tom Restless of *Idler* 48 has long been associated with Thomas Tyers; Hawkins claims that *Idler* 41 was occasioned by the death of Johnson's mother, and Bertrand Bronson has argued that Aspasia in *Irene* is an idealized portrait of Johnson's wife *(Johnson Agonistes and Other Essays)*. Many general discussions in Johnson's works—of the plight of authors in the periodical essays, of the student in *The Vanity of Human Wishes,* for example— are of compelling personal significance. Boswell points out what he perceives (sometimes correctly, sometimes not) to be traces of Johnson's own personality in the *Lives of the Poets (Life)*. The sense of personal urgency is beyond question in a passage such as Johnson's discussion of the outset of Shakespeare's career:

> He came to London a needy adventurer, and lived for a time by very mean employments. Many works of genius and learning have been performed in states of life, that appear very little favourable to thought or to enquiry; so many, that he who considers them is inclined to think that he sees enterprise and perseverance predominating over all external agency, and bidding help and hindrance vanish before them. The genius of Shakespeare was not to be depressed by the weight of poverty, nor limited by the narrow conversation to which men in want are inevitably condemned.
>
> *(Johnson on Shakespeare)*

In his early biographical sketch of Lewis Morin, the French botanist and physician (1741), Johnson views the slow advance but eventual triumph of "unassisted merit" (1825 *Works*). There is now general agreement that one of Johnson's most important models was Boerhaave, the Dutch physician whose life he wrote in 1739. Catholic in his interests, modest but firm in the company of the great, subject to numerous forms of physical suffering, Boerhaave's personality and experience closely parallel Johnson's. He too began in poverty, "but with a Resolution equal to his Abilities, and a Spirit not to be depress'd or shaken, he determin'd to break thro' the Obstacles of Poverty, and supply by Diligence the want of Fortune."

It is natural, in such passages as these, to stress Johnson's need for inspiration, reassurance, and constant bolstering, for the self-portrait with which most of us are most fully acquainted is the Johnson of the *Prayers and Meditations:* the tormented individual, resolving to retard his backsliding, determined to rise early, keep a journal, read through scripture annually, and avoid idleness and sloth. Such self-disparagement is an important part of Johnson's process of self-examination. He told Mrs. Piozzi "that the character of *Sober* in the Idler, was . . . intended as his own portrait; and that he had his own outset into life in his eye when he wrote the eastern story of Gelaleddin" *(Anecdotes). Idler* 31 begins with the suggestion that although pride enjoys the "pre-eminence of mischief" idleness provides pride with formidable competition. The chief practitioner of idleness in the essay is Mr. Sober, a man who fills "the day with petty business . . . [and has] always something in hand which may raise curiosity, but not solicitude, and keep the mind in a state of action but not of labour." His "chief pleasure is conversation"; he is terrified at the prospect of solitude and seeks to fill his time with mechanical tinkering. "His daily amusement is chemistry. . . . He . . . sits and counts the drops as they come from his retort, and forgets that, while a drop is falling, a moment flies away." This is severe self-criticism but not, for Johnson, surprising.

The sketch of Gelaleddin in *Idler* 75 continues the pattern, but with significant alterations. Gelaleddin, a young native of Tauris, is described as "amiable in his manners and beautiful in his form, of boundless curiosity, incessant diligence, and irresistible genius, of quick apprehension and tenacious memory, accurate without narrowness, and eager for novelty without inconstancy." The intellectual attributes suggest Johnson, if the physical ones do not. Gelaleddin is offered a professorship at Bassora, but instead seeks wealth and power in Tauris, believing he can always fall back upon "academical obscurity." His expectations are systematically blighted. His father sees him as an additional financial burden. His eloquence impresses neither the poor nor his brothers and sisters, who are preoccupied with their own indigence. He engenders envy among those who frequent "places of publick resort," and receives no employment from the visiers. He finally returns to Bassora where he is treated as "a fugitive, who returned only because he could live in no other place."

Johnson has altered the grounds for self-criticism. Gelaleddin is a victim of naïvéte, not idleness. He is ignorant of the point which Johnson makes at length in the *Journey,* the fact that immediate wants may be so pressing that there is little room left for learning and letters. Gelaleddin is apparently unaware of the tenuous, evanescent nature of worldly fame, the fact that greatness changes as the context which produced it changes. The mature Johnson continually treats these issues; Gelaleddin is learning the implicit lessons firsthand. What is striking in the self-portrait is the introduction of factors which mitigate the self-criticism. Gelaleddin is victimized by innocence, illusion, and ambition but he is also endowed with an imposing list of intellectual and moral strengths. Johnson's admission that he had his own situation in mind when composing the piece hardly suggests self-laceration. Moreover, Gelaleddin's failings are common to the rest of mankind, though his abilities are decidedly uncommon, and his suffering results as much from a world of poverty, envy, and fear, as it does a lack of experience or a culpable desire for "greatness." There is blame here, but praise as well; the balancing of both, in my judgment, constitutes the major characteristic of Johnson's self-portraits.

The best modern commentary on the *Prayers and Meditations* has directed attention to two important matters. The first is the extent to which one falsifies Johnson's work by reading it rapidly. The result is nearly always the sense that Johnson's resolutions and failure to fulfill his own expectations come as swiftly as one can read them. Johnson's psychological stability is called into question without proper basis, for Johnson's self-examinations and resolves were usually keyed to some liturgical event or date with strong personal associations: his birthday, the anniversary of the death of his wife, the beginning of an important project, and, of course, New Year's. Second, Johnson's low assessment of his own achievements does not spring from a lack of awareness of the importance or the difficulty of his completed tasks, but rather from a realization of what he could accomplish, should he determine to do so. He is thoroughly aware of the talents which God has bestowed upon him as well as the fact that much more is, accordingly, demanded of him. Boswell realizes this, even if he does not use it properly:

> The solemn text, "of him to whom much is given, much will
> be required," seems to have been ever present to his mind, in
> a rigorous sense, and to have made him dissatisfied with his labours
> and acts of goodness, however comparatively great; so that the
> unavoidable consciousness of his superiority was, in that respect,
> a cause of disquiet.
>
> *(Life)*

Even George III could appeal to this principle and indicate the responsibilities which attend ability:

Johnson said, he thought he had already done his part as a writer. "I should have thought so too, (said the King,) if you had not written so well."—Johnson observed to me, upon this, that "No man could have paid a handsomer compliment; and it was fit for a King to pay. It was decisive."

(Life)

Pride and humility are simultaneously generated by the parable of the talents; in Johnson they represent complementary sides of a complex human reality. All too often, particularly in the nineteenth century, they have been separated. Stress fell upon Johnson's devastating pride in public, social performances, his abject humility in private, devotional contexts, and both the pride and the humility were judged aberrational. On the one hand there was the conversational titan, carving or bludgeoning the opposition with cleverness and the sheer force of personality, on the other a cringing victim of religious excess, scrupulous to a fault. The pride and humility cannot be separated in this fashion; indeed they are mutually defining and must be seen in tandem, a pattern which frequently appears in Johnson's works.

Although I disagree with some of Lawrence Lipking's conclusions concerning Johnsonian self-portraiture I am in full agreement with his attitude toward its use:

Johnson's writings teem with self-references, with efforts to be acquainted with himself, with moral analysis of his own psychological predicaments. . . . Many Johnsonians carry within them an anthology . . . from which they recreate, moment by moment, a version of Johnson's spiritual autobiography. Why has that anthology not been published? To some extent its absence constitutes the most puzzling omission in the canon of Johnsonian biography. . . . And how remarkable that not one of Johnson's biographers, so far as I can find, has chosen to focus on the moving Latin poem, full of self-doubt and self-analysis, that Johnson wrote upon revising his Dictionary, and gave the Greek title of "Know thyself"! Is it possible that what *Johnson* thought about Johnson counts for so very little?

The poem to which Lipking quite properly refers was completed after the revision for the fourth edition of the Dictionary. Readers of *Idler* 31 will not be surprised by Johnson's sentiments, here quoted in Arthur Murphy's translation:

> My task perform'd, and all my labours o'er,
> For me what lot has Fortune now in store?
> The listless will succeeds, that worst disease,
> The rack of indolence, the sluggish ease.
> Care grows on care, and o'er my aching brain
> Black melancholy pours her morbid train.
> No kind relief, no lenitive at hand,
> I seek at midnight clubs, the social band;
> But midnight clubs, where wit with noise conspires,
> Where Comus revels, and where wine inspires,
> Delight no more; I seek my lonely bed,
> and call on sleep to sooth my languid head. . . .
>
> Whate'er I plan, I feel my pow'rs confin'd
> By Fortune's frown and penury of mind.
> I boast no knowledge glean'd with toil and strife,
> That bright reward of a well-acted life.
> I view myself, while reason's feeble light
> Shoots a pale glimmer through the gloom of night,
> While passions, error, phantoms of the brain
> And vain opinions, fill the dark domain;
> A dreary void, where fears with grief combin'd
> Waste all within, and desolate the mind.
>
> What then remains? Must I in slow decline
> To mute inglorious ease old age resign?
> Or, bold ambition kindling in my breast,
> Attempt some arduous task? Or, were it best
> Brooding o'er lexicons to pass the day,
> And in that labour drudge my life away?
>
> <div align="right">(<i>Poems</i>)</div>

The very act of committing one's mental state to verse is an assertion, and in Johnson's case a powerful one. The indolence of which he writes would be trivial were it not for the magnitude of the task which he has accomplished. The laborious drudgery which he foresees as a possible way of life jostles with his lofty ambitions. The element of pride and self-confidence is most apparent in the poem when we consider the manner in which our response would be altered if Johnson were not its author. If the poem had been written by a hack or poetaster after the completion of a now forgotten work, we would consider it mannered, pretentious posturing. The success of the poem turns on the stature of its author.

In similar fashion Johnson may term his lexicographic task the work of "a harmless drudge," but in the final paragraph of the Dictionary's Preface he turns to autobiographical concerns and assumes a stance of near-heroic indifference, maintaining a fragile balance between arrogance and high nobility:

> The *English Dictionary* was written with little assistance of the learned, and without any patronage of the great; not in the soft obscurities of retirement, or under the shelter of academick bowers, but amidst inconvenience and distraction, in sickness and in sorrow. It may repress the triumph of malignant criticism to observe, that if our language is not here fully displayed, I have only failed in an attempt which no human powers have hitherto completed. . . .
>
> . . . I have protracted my work till most of those whom I wished to please have sunk into the grave, and success and miscarriage are empty sounds: I therefore dismiss it with frigid tranquillity, having little to fear or hope from censure or from praise.

Commenting on the work of the literary scholar in the *Preface to Shakespeare,* Johnson writes that "the subjects to be discussed by him are of very small importance; they involve neither property nor liberty; nor favour the interest of sect or party" (*Johnson on Shakespeare*). However, Johnson's pride complements his humility, for Pope's comments on "the dull duty of an editor" bring a swift rejoinder: "Conjectural criticism demands more than humanity possesses, and he that exercises it with most praise has very frequent need of indulgence. Let us now be told no more of the dull duty of an editor."

In *The Vision of Theodore* Johnson assumes the role of adviser and boldly counsels the youthful readers of Dodsley's *Preceptor*—in which the work appeared—concerning such weighty issues as the relation between Reason and Religion and the nature of human motivation. Yet when he, in the allegory, describes the "Maze of Indolence" which ends in the dominion of Melancholy, who finally consigns her prisoners to the cruel control of Despair, we sense an intense portrayal of personal religious experience which is highly self-critical. In the *Journey* Johnson assumes the role of Enlightenment empiricist, challenging Scottish credulity; at the same time he admits his own shortcomings, the opportunities he has missed and facts he has forgotten. He dictates to the Scots concerning the cultivation (in the broadest sense) of their lands and people but is able, simultaneously, to portray himself with humility and gentle humor:

> Here I first mounted a little Highland steed; and if there had been many spectators, should have been somewhat ashamed of my figure in the march. The horses of the Islands, as of other barren countries, are very low: they are indeed musculous and strong, beyond what their size gives reason for expecting; but a bulky man upon one of their backs makes a very disproportionate appearance.
>
> *(Journey)*

In the *Rambler* Johnson toys with the image of the eidolon which he has himself created. Mr. Rambler's fondness for gloom, wretchedness, and hard words is lamented by fictional correspondents. The humor turns on Johnson's awareness and exploitation of his carefully constructed short-comings and perversities, a process roughly paralleling his parodying of his own "prejudices" in light conversation. He jettisons Steele's paradigm of the social commentator and moral adviser as a man of near flawless virtue and offers his own alternative. In *Rambler* 155 he indicates that the giving of advice involves an implicit claim of superiority which generally proves unpalatable and, finally, inefficacious. As Shaftesbury put it, the free gift of advice takes from another and adds to ourself *(Characteristics).* Some degree of superiority, on the other hand, would seem to be necessary, for, as Johnson writes in *Ramber* 14, "men would not more patiently submit to be taught, than commanded, by one known to have the same follies and weaknesses with themselves." The ideal would be an adviser who can serve as an example as well. Because the number of such individuals is miniscule, Steele and his legion of imitators generally constructed idealized eidolons who were largely separated from their creators. Johnson, on the other hand, has been attacked for blurring the author/eidolon line. In point of fact Johnson's practice suggests that of Montaigne rather than Addison and Steele. Although there are halfhearted attempts to separate Mr. Rambler from Johnson, they are actually very much alike. Johnson's eidolon combines pride and humility. He possesses authority but he is sufficiently fallen to alleviate any qualms concerning hypocrisy. His task is twofold. He must exhibit the humility which he recommends throughout the periodical as an alternative to vanity and vain desire, yet maintain a sufficient degree of self-assurance to bring his points home without dissipating them in a flood of modesty and timidity. This explains, I think, much of the running dialogue with the audience in which Mr. Rambler informs them of his awareness of his unpopularity but his determination to push on and conduct matters in his own way. He admits that he lacks certain strengths and must capitalize on those he does possess. He confesses shortcomings but maintains his courage. He displays warmth but also independence, insecurity (to an extent) but also confidence. The same figure who humbly writes that he has "never been much a favourite of the publick" (no. 208), can also announce that "the men who can be charged with fewest failings, either with respect to abilities or virtue, are generally most ready to allow them." (no. 31)

The praise/blame, pride/humility pattern may appear in secular contexts but its basis, for Johnson, is religious. Joseph Towers summarizes the pattern precisely:

> When the great intellectual powers that Dr. Johnson possessed are considered, and the rapidity with which he finished his compositions, when he could prevail on himself to sit down to write, little doubt can be entertained, but that he might have produced much more than he did; and it was probably this consciousness that occasioned his frequent self-reproaches.

John Wain writes that "Johnson's sense of his own intellectual and spiritual power was a torture to him. For, if much had been given to him, correspondingly much would be asked. The parable of the steward who let his talent lie unused . . . was terrible to him" (*Samuel Johnson*). On Johnson's completion of tasks Hawkins comments that

> this remission of his labour, which seemed to be no more than nature herself called for, Johnson, in those severe audits to which it was his practice to summon himself, would frequently condemn, styling it a waste of his time, and a misapplication of the talents with which he was gratefully conscious that God had endowed him.

> (*Life*)

Haller notes the importance of the parable for the Puritans: "No part of the Puritan code was more weighted with practical significance than this" (*The Rise of Puritanism*). However, Johnson can be far more severe than the Puritans. Milton may be correct in his nineteenth sonnet when he writes that "God doth not need / Either man's work or his own gifts" but Johnson would argue that He still demands them and is far less comfortable than Milton with the notion of standing and waiting. In this general context at least, Wain's judgment that Milton "was in some ways less Puritan than Johnson" (*Johnson as Critic*) is accurate.

The parable of the talents is closely linked with a double vision of man which is profoundly Christian, the notion that our misery and our greatness are near allied. Our accomplishments remind us of our heavenly connections, our failures of our earthly ones. In a sense our pride and humility are not only mutually defining but inseparable. John Dunne treats this pattern in the works of Pascal, Luther, and Erasmus (*A Search for God in Time and Memory*), but the thesis statement is most often drawn from Pascal:

> Christianity is strange. It bids man recognize that he is vile, yea, abominable, and it bids him try to be like God. Without that counterpoise, such an uplift would render him horribly vain, or the humiliation would render him terribly abject.
>
> Christianity then teaches men these twin truths together: that there is a God whom men can reach, and that there is a corruption in their nature which renders them unworthy of Him. Knowledge of both these points is equally important for man; and it is equally dangerous for man to know God without knowing his own misery, and to know his misery without knowing the Redeemer who can cure it. Knowledge of one alone causes either the pride of philosophers who have known God but not their misery, or the despair of atheists who know their misery but not their Redeemer.

The eighteenth century would be particularly aware of this part of Pascal's thought, for the fragmentary version of the *Pensées* which would be in most common use, Kennet's, organizes Pascal's thoughts in a series of chapters, several of which are germane to the issue of man's double nature:

> III: The true Religion proved by the Contrarieties which are discoverable in Man, and by the Doctrine of Original Sin.
> XXI: The strange Contrarieties discoverable in Human Nature, with regard to Truth and Happiness, and many other Things.
> XXIII: The Greatness of Man.
> XXIV: The Vanity of Man.

Johnson's regard for Pascal is well known; he shares the view of human nature which Pascal articulates and realizes that the simultaneous sense of power and impotence, of pride and humility, is intensified in the individual whose gifts are most uncommon. There is an unsettling dynamism built into the Christian life. The more one does the more he realizes how much is left undone. The more one aspires to goodness the more he is conscious of weakness. As Johnson tells Boswell, "The better a man is, the more afraid he is of death, having a clearer view of infinite purity" (*Life*). Such a Christian can never aspire to rest or contentment within the confines of this world and is doomed to the restlessness of which Augustine writes, a restlessness of crucial thematic importance in Johnson's work, particularly in *Rasselas*.

The parable of the talents is an essential part of a vision of history as well as a vision of human nature. The relation between our abilities and accomplishments suggests our simultaneous grandeur and depravity. Both are epitomized in the Incarnation. Man is important enough for God to send His only Son into our midst; man is so pitiful that nothing short of the coming of the Son of God can save him. Within the Christian vision, the historical event of the Incarnation is intimately bound up with notions of human nature. John Dunne writes that "the story of God among men as a man, persuading and dissuading yet not compelling, is perhaps our best clue to what God is and what man is" (*The Way of All the Earth*). In the dramatic, right-angled Christian vision of history, treated so well by Professor Abrams in *Natural Supernaturalism,* the Incarnation is a staggering event. Jung comments:

> The Christian's ordinary conception of God is of an omnipotent, omniscient, and all-merciful Father and Creator of the world. If this God wishes to become man, an incredible *kenosis* (emptying) is required of Him, in order to reduce His totality to the infinitesimal human scale. Even then it is hard to see why the human frame is not shattered by the incarnation. . . . The Christian God-image cannot become incarnate in empirical man without contradictions.
>
> (*Memories, Dreams, Reflections*)

Man, who would imitate Christ, that is, divinity, finds Christ becoming man. Dunne writes that

> When we make humanity our aim . . . and enter thereby into a sympathetic understanding of the passion of Christ, we discover that the fulfilled or hardened or detached being that we had imagined to be divine on the basis of our own desire to be God is not the genuine God, but the genuine God is the one who loses himself as God in order that man may be born.
>
> (*A Search for God in Time and Memory*)

To aspire to divinity is to aspire to full humanity, as Blake—for whom the parable of the talents was also of compelling importance—tells us again and again. "Therefore God becomes as we are, that we may be as he is" (*THERE is NO Natural Religion,* b).

What is particularly striking in all this is the manner in which Johnsonian practice accommodates a crucial portion of eighteenth-century theory. A life-writer's work must be of benefit to his reader, the exemplary value of the work partly turning on the extent to which the biographical subject's experience can be generalized. Despite all of the particular details and contexts of Johnsonian self-portraiture, the way to a larger context is always before us, and in a sense the context is the most important of all, the mutually defining relation of man to God. Jung writes that "although we human beings have our own personal life, we are yet in large measure the representatives, the victims and promoters of a collective spirit whose years are counted in centuries" (*Memories, Dreams, Reflections*) and Goethe argues that "every one must form himself as a particular being, seeking, however, to attain that general idea of which all mankind are constituents" (Eckermann, *Words of Goethe*).

Each human life recapitulates common human experience. The result for life-writing very often is an element of structural predictability so that even the vivid, particularized account of which Johnson is capable has certain affinities with forms as stylized as saints' lives, criminal biographies, and Puritan autobiographies. In Johnson's self-portraits we immediately confront a larger pattern, and the differences between Johnson and Boswell in this regard are important. The relationships which interest Boswell are those of man to land, family, class, and position. Boswell stresses these patterns in Johnson, excessively in my judgment, while failing to come to terms with the pattern which, for Johnson, is of paramount importance, the relation of man to God. Boswell suffers because he perceives life as mystery rather than as paradox. He seeks to understand, while Johnson seeks to cope. The problem for Johnson is not one of understanding, but of dealing with a situation which is intelligible but which, at the outset, removes the possibility of rest and contentment. Thus Johnson is impatient with Boswellian melancholy, partly because Boswell is self-indulgent with it, but chiefly because it is of a lower order than his own.

I would not argue that the pride and humility which result from Johnson's intense awareness of the parable of the talents are sufficient unto themselves as a biographer's "image," that is, more would be necessary if one were writing Johnson's life. This pattern is a very important one and explains a great deal but it is, obviously, a very general pattern. The "image" which emerges from modern scholarship might be something like this:

> Samuel Johnson. Englishman from Staffordshire, of middle class parentage, respectable but poor. He moves from trying familial and financial positions to success as a professional writer. Essentially, he is a moralist and hortatory psychologist, an energetic and incisive scholar. He is one of the few post-Renaissance prose writers who writes in a recognizable style; he is an accomplished poet, one whose verse has still not received the attention it deserves. He is perhaps the greatest literary critic who has ever lived but one who is, in the best sense of the word, unsystematic. He gives his name to his age but he is not always of that age. He dislikes much eighteenth-century literature and is fundamentally at odds with the spirit and practice of satire. He lambasts such brahmins as Pope, Swift, and Gray and prefers biography at a time when it is seldom written with great effectiveness. He is a rebellious conservative who espouses Tory and High Church norms in an age of Whigs and skeptics; his allegiance, however, is always to the eternal. His norms are never strictly partisan. He is willing to attack anyone when Christian norms are violated. He is in tune with all of the fundamental tenets of the Enlightenment except for its libertinism and antireligious skepticism. For all of his uniqueness, to himself he is everyman. His own image for himself, a mixture of pride and humility, turns on the importance of the parable of the talents within the Christian vision and it is the general nature of this pattern which seizes his attention. He is both a human being and a quasi-fictional character in a great book. Largely because of that book, he is a crucial part of Western consciousness, but not always for the right reasons. His works justify that position, but their role—chiefly because of Boswell and the tradition he initiates—has all too often been a subservient one.

A brief sketch such as this does not begin to touch on the varied aspects of Johnson's experience. I include it only to highlight some of the interests of Johnson's modern students and indicate, by implication, a part of the disparity between our Johnson and Boswell's. It could be argued that "images" of Johnson may be traced in the *Life,* "images" which I have not treated. In a sense that is true. There are repeating references to Johnson which follow certain patterns, for example, Johnson as modern Hercules or Socrates, but such images usually serve to elucidate certain facets of Johnson's personality as Boswell perceives them. For an overarching, sophisticated image based on an awareness of the available material, an image which is used systematically to organize materials for the reader, one looks, in my judgment, in vain.

Boswell's vision of Johnson's life consists, essentially, of a series of images: Johnson in conversation, Johnson in encounters, Johnson in "scenes." The pattern suggests the pictorialist tradition of which Jean Hagstrum writes (*The Sister Arts*), a tradition which in poetry generates structures which suggest picture galleries. Such poetry, "in which we move from scene to scene, tableau to tableau" is a kind of "pageant with interpretative comment." A poem (or biography) like this "is a *display* of personages whose mental and physical measure is being taken and who reveal their character in what they are seen to be and heard to say." In the *London Journal* Boswell recounts some comments made by Dempster:

> He considered the mind of man like a room, which is either made agreeable or the reverse by the pictures with which it is adorned. External circumstances are nothing to the purpose. Our great point is to have pleasing pictures in the inside. . . . The great art is to have an agreeable collection to preserve them well.

Boswell comments, "This is really an ingenious and lively fancy. . . . [As a man] grows up, he gets some substantial pieces which he always preserves, although he may alter his smaller paintings in a moment." This, it seems to me, is an excellent introduction to the manner in which Boswell shapes' experience and there is no question that many of his "substantial pieces" were to be pictures of Johnson. As we read such works as Johnson's "Annals" we find that *his* sense of experience is fluid and varied. Thousands of details, each rich with associations, combine in his memory and constitute his identity. From the man-midwife Hector's "Here is a brave boy!" to his final "GOD bless you, my dear!" the elements in Johnson's memory would lead in one of two directions: either to a multivolumed autobiography, encyclopedic in scope and nearly so in length, or to a single image which would depict Johnson's striving to utilize his talents and imitate his Lord, a picture like Blake's of Albion standing with outstretched arms before the crucified Christ. Boswell's memories are beautifully, poignantly, and appropriately portrayed as a series of scenes in a play or pictures in a gallery, few in number but each of vast importance; Johnson's are not.

Factual Appearances and Fictional Effects: Boswell's *Life of Johnson*

William R. Siebenschuh

For over a century Boswell's *Life of Johnson* was considered a monument to assiduous fact-gathering and remarkable, near-verbatim transcription of Johnson's conversation. Since the discovery of Boswell's private papers, however, there has been a steady erosion of the image of Boswell as fact-gatherer and recorder. It is clear now that he was a conscious artist; that he exercised a substantial amount of control over the image of Johnson that his book creates; and that in portraying Johnson he depended heavily on techniques we normally associate with fiction. With these discoveries of the extent of Boswell's literary art have come serious reservations about the value of the *Life* as accurate biography. The crux of the matter has been stated concisely by Richard Schwartz. "In Boswell's biography of Johnson," he writes, "a real individual is portrayed. The portrayal, however, is such that Boswell's protagonist takes on many of the trappings of a fictional character. The problem in this situation is of a normative one: is the exemplary value of a historical personage enhanced or diminished by the introduction of techniques associated with fiction?" This, in simplified form, is the question I address here, although it is a matter of much present controversy and involves conflicting schools of thought. Some scholars still maintain essentially traditional views about the historical validity of Boswell's record and, with some concession to recent studies of his art, do not accept the notion that his Johnson is fictional in any of the senses now being proposed.

Others, like Schwartz, assert flatly that the portrait of Johnson in the *Life* is not biography at all, that instead it is autobiography and, as Donald Greene suggests, that the Johnson we meet in the *Life* is an essentially fictional creation of Boswell's, a "character in his book." A few critics, however, approach the *Life* without denying the existence of the art, assuming that its presence automatically compromises biographical truth, or dichotomizing and discussing art and fact separately. Ralph Rader argues, for instance, that the *Life* successfully "transcends while fulfilling the usual purpose of history and biography, to provide true knowledge of the human past." Boswell does this, Rader says, by "raising his subject [by means of his art] constructively out of the past and representing [it] to the imagination as a concrete, self-intelligible cause of emotion." More recently, William C. Dowling has approached the question from a slightly different direction. "Boswell's great subject," he says, "is the hero in an unheroic world. To speak of the Boswellian hero is really to speak of a certain dramatic situation that is explored in a different way in each of [Boswell's] narratives, one which takes the simple figure of the hero as the symbolic focus of larger and more complex moral concerns." Dowling uses the word *hero* in a highly specific sense. He argues that Boswell's achievement in the *Life* is best understood when we fully appreciate its affinities to the "bios" tradition and the traditions of heroic literature and myth. In Dowling's view, Boswell makes Johnson a symbol of old values in "an age where reason has gone to war with faith, where abstract theories of social progress have triumphed over an older wisdom of tradition and continuity [represented by Johnson], and where society has become the enemy of the free self." In this sense, Dowling does an excellent job of attempting to give flesh and bones to Rader's idea that Boswell's Johnson is an "objective correlative of a grand emotive idea."

Dowling's book, *The Boswellian Hero*, is especially important to this study because more than most recent Boswellian critics other than Rader, Dowling attempts a comprehensive literary explanation for Boswell's biographical achievement, and in doing so he inevitably confronts the question that concerns me here: how is our response to the portrait of Johnson in the *Life* affected by Boswell's use of techniques we usually associate with fiction? Dowling responds obliquely to this question. Whereas Rader argues that the portrait transcends while fulfilling the ordinary purposes of biography, Dowling suggests that in the course of the current debate about the generic status of the portrait of Johnson in the *Life*

> art and history, coherence and correspondence, have . . . been
> placed in false conflict. They are not qualities of biography, but

aspects in which biography can be seen, in much the same way as we can look at a Greek vase both as an expression of man's visual imagination and as a thing for carrying water. The consequences are obvious: to read the *Life of Johnson* as literature is only to begin where all criticism must begin, with an awareness of its self-contained nature as a work of art—something that is in no way inconsistent with its being a repository of facts about the 'real' Samuel Johnson.

The generic status of the portrait of Johnson in the *Life* depends, according to Dowling, on the "universe of discourse" in which we approach it.

As I have argued in general above, I believe along with Dowling that in a case like the portrait of Johnson in the *Life*, "art and history, coherence and correspondence have been placed in false conflict," but not precisely for the reason he suggests. Although, of course, the *Life* can have any number of separate existences—as a work of art, a repository of facts, or a historical or sociological document—to argue thus is to miss an important point that I shall try to make here. In my view, one does not need to argue simultaneous generic existence (like that of Dowling's Greek vase) to defend the existence of Boswell's art. The art, I believe, *is* the biographical statement—not in a separate universe of discourse, but in the same universe of discourse. Boswell's art in the *Life* cannot be separated from interpretive biographical statement any more than Newman's art can be divorced from his autobiographical statement in the *Apologia*.

My attempt to prove this assertion will, of necessity, take me in directions in which Dowling did not have to go. Because he assumes simultaneous states of generic existence, Dowling concentrates on statements made by Boswell's art without closely pursuing questions of, for example, discrepancies between original journal records and the final text in the *Life*. Because I shall argue that in the *Life* artistic choice is valid interpretive biographical statement, I cannot avoid this issue. Given his premises, Dowling does not need to confront old questions about the role of apparently unassimilable factual data in a heroic portrait or about the role of dramatic art in a factual work (generic problems with which critics of fictional heroic works like the *Odyssey* and the *Aeneid* do not have to deal). Given his premises, Dowling need not confront recent questions of Boswell's suppression or distortion of his primary material; from Dowling's point of view this is presumably a problem in another universe of discourse. It is, however, an issue that must concern me directly.

Given my own premises, the closer one looks at Boswell's text the harder it is to describe, let alone assess, his achievements. According to traditional definitions, one cannot safely categorize his art as either literal transcription or invention, or as simply good drama or good biography. In many instances we have Boswell's original journal records of episodes that are substantially rewritten for inclusion in the *Life*. The changes he makes when writing the versions in the *Life* are often major. Sometimes he alters his records of Johnson's conversation; sometimes he describes his reactions and role in an episode one way in the journals and another way in the *Life*. He omits and selects material and controls our reaction continuously.

A well-known, concrete example—Boswell's treatment of his first meeting with Johnson—makes the nature of the problem clearer, and it is worth studying in detail. For anyone whose familiarity with this moment is based solely on the account of it in the *Life*, reading the original version in the *London Journal, 1762–1763* must be something of a disappointment. The same basic factual skeleton is there but none of the drama and little of the sense of momentousness. On Monday, May 16, 1763, Boswell records in his journal that

> Temple and his brother breakfasted with me. I went to Love's to try to recover some of the money which he owes me. But, alas, a single guinea was all I could get. He was just going to dinner, so I stayed and eat a bit, though I was angry at myself afterwards. I drank tea at Davies in Russell Street, and about seven came in the great Mr. Samuel Johnson, whom I have so long wished to see. Mr. Davies introduced me to him. As I knew his mortal antipathy to the Scotch, I cried to Davies, "Don't tell where I come from." However, he said, "From Scotland." "Mr. Johnson," said I, "indeed I come from Scotland, but I cannot help it." "Sir," replied he, "that, I find, is what a very great many of your countrymen cannot help." Mr. Johnson is a man of a most dreadful appearance. He is a very big man, is troubled with sore eyes, the palsy, and the King's evil. He is very slovenly in his dress and speaks with a most uncouth voice. Yet his great knowledge and strength of expression command vast respect and render him excellent company. He has a great humour and is a worthy man. But his dogmatical roughness of manners is disagreeable. I shall mark what I remember of his conversation.

Boswell then goes on to list a relatively short series of separate remarks that he remembers Johnson to have made: about some differences between barbarous and more polished times, about Lord Kames's *Elements*, about Wilkes and the notion of liberty, and about Thomas Sheridan. He concludes the episode by saying, "I was sorry to leave him there at ten, when I had engaged to be at Dr. Pringle's with whom I had a serious conversation much to my mind." That is it. The journal record flows on undisturbed. Apparently no earthshaking impact has been made on the journalist, nothing that even approximates the impression we get from the account in the *Life*.

When Boswell was writing the *Life*, he was seeing the moment in retrospect, and there he makes it a symbolic episode. He is also writing Johnson's biography, and so he makes interpretive comment by means of dramatic effects. In the *Life* he carefully prepares for our experience of the meeting, and he gives us a focused context in which to view it. Boswell begins the record of the year 1763 by announcing: "This is to me a memorable year; for in it I had the happiness to obtain the acquaintance of that extraordinary man whose memoirs I am now writing; an acquaintance which I shall ever esteem as one of the most fortunate circumstances of my life."

Although in the *London Journal* he had "long wished to see Johnson," he makes a capsule version of the full story of his search an integral part of the episode in the *Life*. "Though then but two-and-twenty," he continues, "I had for several years read his works with delight and instruction, and had the highest reverence for their author, which had grown up in my fancy into a mysterious veneration, by figuring to myself a state of solemn elevated abstraction, in which I had supposed him to live in the immense metropolis of London."

In the version in the *Life*, Boswell encourages us to experience vicariously the story of his pursuit of Johnson. It is a masterpiece of narrative technique: a succession of near misses, excitement, expectation, disappointment, and, at last, success. First he thinks Derrick will get him an introduction, but this never materializes. Then there is a chance that Sheridan will be able to arrange a meeting, but Johnson's unlucky remark ("What, have they given [Sheridan] a pension? Then it is time for me to give up mine.") makes this impossible. At this point Boswell discusses the Sheridan episode and Sheridan himself for more than two pages, and this is exactly the sort of thing for which he has been criticized: the inclusion of apparently wholly tangential material into the *Life*. It is the kind of practice that has been used in the past to demonstrate a lack of controlling artistry or broad organizational abilities. Yet if we were reading a novel we would immediately recognize a fairly standard ploy. The narrator announces that some great event is just about to happen, then temporarily slows the pace to build suspense.

At last we come to Davies—the man who will finally bring the two together. He provides fresh hope that at first produces only a series of new disappointments. The actual meeting occurs by chance. "At last," says Boswell at the dramatically optimum moment, "on Monday the 16th of May, when I was sitting in Mr. Davies back parlour, after having drunk tea with him and Mrs. Davies, Johnson unexpectedly came into the shop; and Mr. Davies having perceived him through the glass-door in the room in which we were sitting, advancing toward us, he announced his aweful approach to me, somewhat in the manner of an actor in the part of Horatio, when he addresses Hamlet on the appearance of his father's ghost, 'Look, my Lord, it comes.'"

In the journal we have only the remark that "about seven came in the great Mr. Samuel Johnson whom I have so long wished to see." In the *Life* Boswell constantly manipulates our point of view. At first we see Johnson through Davies's eyes as Johnson is bearing down on Boswell from behind. The reference to the glass door helps us visualize the scene and heightens the drama. The allusion to *Hamlet* is perfect here. It works in the same way it would have worked had it been made in a novel or a play because it becomes a focal point for several related impressions that Boswell wants to create. Given the state of mind Boswell has described himself as being in, Johnson (like the ghost for Hamlet) is a kingly figure whom he wants to meet very much and yet who is distant, majestic, awesome, and, to some, terrifying. Avoiding the intrusion of clumsy formal commentary, the allusion makes us imaginatively aware of all its implications and simultaneously and subtly enlarges Johnson for us. An important omission follows.

In the *Life* Boswell never mentions his actual reaction to Johnson's "dreadful" appearance. This is one of the clearest indications that he is consciously trying to control *our* reaction to Johnson. There is no mention of the sore eyes, the palsy, or the King's evil. He does mention Johnson's appearance, though, by observing that he found that he had a perfect idea of Johnson's figure "from the portrait of him painted by Sir Joshua Reynolds soon after he had published his *Dictionary*, in the attitude of sitting in his easy chair in deep meditation."

How familiar Boswell's readers would have been with the various portraits of Johnson is hard to guess. Boswell's reference here is to the portrait readers would have seen as a frontispiece to the *Life*; it is a flattering allusion in much the same way the allusion to Hamlet is. The portrait to which Boswell refers captures Johnson's massiveness and rough features, but it also throws a great deal of emphasis on his studious, contemplative side. A later portrait by Reynolds (with which Boswell was probably familiar) shows

Johnson standing. The rough contours of his face, a face that appears to be in pain, his eyes weakened and half closed, his hands either half clenched or in a gesture of supplication, seem closer to the Johnson who created Boswell's initial impression.

His treatment of the conversation that occurred on that famous day is in keeping with the other alterations of the original record described above. The nugget that most people carry away from the meeting is Johnson's remark about Boswell's coming from Scotland. In the *London Journal* Boswell simply records the dialogue. In the *Life* the account is much fuller, and Johnson's famous retort does not follow immediately. Here Boswell, as he invariably does, generalizes from the reply to a greater fact about Johnson's character. "I am willing," he says,

> to flatter myself that I meant this as light pleasantry to sooth and conciliate him, and not as an humiliating abasement at the expense of my country. But however that might be, this speech was somewhat unlucky; for with that quickness of wit for which he was so remarkable, he seized the expression 'come from Scotland,' which I used in the sense of being of that country, and as if I had said that I had come away from it, or left it, retorted, "That, Sir, I find is what a great many of your countrymen cannot help."

Boswell goes on from here to attempt to elbow his way into the conversation about Garrick. This move results in the stern rebuff by Johnson. "Sir, . . . I have known David Garrick longer than you have done; and I know no right you have to talk to me on the subject." Boswell is taken aback, but recovers, repeats the snatches of conversation that are essentially the same as those in the *London Journal*, and then concludes the episode with some important parting observations that do not appear in the original record. "I was highly pleased," he writes in the *Life*,

> with the extraordinary vigour of his conversation, and regretted that I was drawn away from it by an engagement at another place. I had, for part of the evening, been left alone with him, and had ventured to make an observation now and then, which he received very civilly; so that I was satisfied that though there was roughness in his manner, there was no ill-nature in his disposition. Davies followed me to the door, and when I complained a little of the hard blows which the great man had given me, he kindly took upon him to console me by saying, "Don't be uneasy, I can see he likes you very well."

In the *London Journal* Boswell had observed that Johnson's "dogmatical roughness of manner was disagreeable" and concluded only by noting that he was "sorry to leave at ten, when I had engaged to be at Dr. Pringle's, with whom I had a serious conversation much to my mind."

Obviously Boswell made a great many changes when he expanded the original journal record, and it is important to note carefully what those changes were. They involved, primarily, additions to the original record, not omissions (with the exception of Boswell's reaction to Johnson's appearance). And although Boswell dresses up Johnson's language in the way that he is known to have done systematically throughout the *Life*, the major changes do not involve Johnson but Boswell himself. He makes his own role and reactions a more important part of the account in the *Life*, and the changes are aimed at us. If they do not alter the central core of Johnsonian record, they dramatically affect the way we react to it.

In writing the episode for the *Life*, Boswell uses himself in the way a novelist might use a narrator. One of his primary goals as a biographer is to prevent our reacting to Johnson's rough appearance and dogmatic manner as he did himself at first. Since we are going to see Johnson here "more completely than any man who has yet lived," Boswell wants to make sure that we get beyond the rugged exterior and well-known combustibility and see the greatness and the goodness beneath. Thus, as he does so often in the *Life*, he makes the episode into a tiny symbolic action with beginning, middle, and end. First there is the desired meeting with Johnson; then surprise, even consternation at his remarkable appearance; then, finally, the delightful discovery of the powers of his mind and his essential kindness, wisdom, and good nature. Boswell repeats this pattern in many forms, and it is in this context that the Garrick outburst is important—for Boswell did not mention it formally in the original record.

At first glance, the Garrick episode seems to contradict the impression Boswell wants to create. Until it occurs, Boswell has only been tossed playfully by Johnson, but this nearly crushes him: "I now felt myself much mortified, and began to think that the hope which I had long indulged of obtaining his acquaintance was blasted. And, in truth, had not my ardour been uncommonly strong, and my resolution uncommonly persevering, such a reception might have deterred me for ever from making any further attempts."

Boswell wants us to see the importance of the ultimate reconciliation. He perseveres and Johnson rewards him not only with consideration but with friendship. "Don't be uneasy," Davies tells him as he leaves, "I can see he likes you very well." This bit of dialogue does not occur in the original, although it is not impossible that Davies did say it and that Boswell remembered it years later. Whatever the case, he dramatically positions it here to make the point that he will be at great pains to continue to make: Johnson was a great man, not a great bear.

The changes Boswell makes in writing this version in the *Life* are typical, but they by no means represent the full spectrum of alterations, omissions, and artistic choices the *Life* as a whole contains. Still, this example is more than sufficient to raise the sorts of questions that are now being raised about the validity of calling the *Life* biography. The version of this first meeting is clearly better drama in the *Life* than in the journal. Is it legitimate for Boswell to downplay his reaction to Johnson's appearance at the time in order to make it consistent with his feelings in retrospect? Although Boswell has the rare authority to dramatize that we normally concede only to biographers who know their subjects, is it permissible for him to use versions of himself in the way that novelists sometimes use ficitional narrators? Is it fair, that is, to try to create reactions in us that were not typical of the biographer himself—and that he does not tell us he is trying to create? Does that not verge on rewriting history—or on fiction?

These, and more, are the hard questions Boswell's book now invites. I believe they can be answered satisfactorily, but before they can be addressed sensibly, we need to have a clear and complete picture of Boswell's art in the *Life*. I attempt to supply this below where I argue, ultimately, that although Boswell's portrait of Johnson is limited and incomplete in many senses, Boswell's achievement represents a nearly perfect compromise between the power of his literary art and the generic demands of the biographical form in which he writes.

Obviously Boswell's art is much easier to deal with if we consider it only as literary art and thus somehow separable from the biographical statements he uses it to make. When we consider it as biographical statement, we encounter a major problem: Boswell's best art in the *Life* conceals itself. (Although Dowling may quite correctly place Boswell's treatment of Johnson within a well-known heroic and/or biographical tradition, it is commonplace to observe that until our century Boswell's scrupulous adherence to fact was seldom if ever questioned and that he was considered a brilliant "recorder" and, if one accepted Macaulay's view, an artist by accident or good luck.) To a degree far in excess of either Newman or Gosse, Boswell disguises the relation between his art, his evidence, and his interpretive statements. As everyone knows, he does everything in his power consistently to create the impression of total candor and slavish attention to factual accuracy. In a famous passage he tells us that he has sometimes run half way across London in order to fix a date. Formally, he claims that he is setting the record straight—correcting the errors or misconceptions of others. Yet a close look at the actual relation between the facade of total inclusion of factual data, the impression he creates that he has exercised total candor in representing Johnson, and Boswell's controlling purpose as interpretive artist-biographer reveals a systematic and highly sophisticated use of the apparent nature and limitations of the factual genres and of the genres' components in order to amplify uniquely the effects of his art.

Boswell's treatment of Johnson's oddities and appearance is a good example of his methods in general. Our sense of Johnson's physical appearance, habitual gestures, and frequent bull-in-a-china-shop effect on polite society have always been among the great legacies of the *Life*. Rather than repelling us from Johnson, they are the rough edges to which many cling quite happily and not without good reason. Dowling suggests, quite correctly I believe, that they add to our sense of Johnson's heroism because "they reveal the precise degree to which the real relation of the hero to his society . . . is disharmonious." What concerns me here is the degree to which Boswell makes us believe we are seeing Johnson "warts and all" when, in fact, what we are seeing is a carefully controlled image.

Boswell obviously felt from the beginning that he could not describe Johnson's appearance in detail without risk. Too great an impression made by the oddities and singularities might detract from his concentration on Johnson's inner greatness. These instincts were probably correct. Other contemporary biographies suggest this strongly, at any rate. There is no reason to believe that most (certainly many) of Johnson's other biographers did not at the very least admire him, but their physical descriptions of him are far from flattering and would jar noticeably if inserted directly into the text of the *Life*. For Sir John Hawkins, for example, "it was, at no time of his life, pleasing to see him at a meal; the greediness with which he ate . . . at the instant degraded him, and shewed him to be more a sensualist than a philosopher. To G. Kearsley, his face "was composed of large, coarse features, which, from a studious turn, when composed, looked sluggish yet awful and contemplative. . . . Though strong, broad, and muscular, his parts were slovenly put together." Of his conversation Letitia Hawkins writes, "Johnson's compliments were studied, and therefore lost their effect: his head dipped lower; the semicircle in which it revolved was of greater extent; and his roar was deeper in its tone when he meant to be civil." From Miss Frances

Reynolds we learn that "It was not only at the entrance of a Door that he exhibited his gigantic straddles but often in the middle of a Room, as if trying to make the floor shake;" but "the manoeuvre that used the most particularly to engage the attention of the company was his stretching out his arm with a full cup of tea in his hand, in every direction, often to the great annoyance of the person who sat next him; . . . sometimes he would twist himself round with his face close to the back of his chair, and finish his cup of tea, breathing very hard, as if making a laborious effort to accomplish it."

These reporters are Johnson's friends (or at least not his enemies). From others he fared much worse. Such glimpses are inherently interesting and recur sufficiently to make it clear that in his own day Johnson was occasionally somewhat of a spectacle. He was not uniformly revered in the way Boswell revered him (and makes us do); and even close friends could be detached enough for occasional irreverence or personal criticism of a sort that never surfaces from Boswell's pages. But if we really want to see Johnson as his valet or as a chance observer must have seen him, we must go to biographers other than Boswell. If we want, on the other hand, the impression that we are seeing him warts and all while instead our assent is being gained to a cumulative image of his greatest strengths and his meaning for us— then we must go to Boswell above all others because he does much more than simply generalize Johnson's peculiarities to one of his greater strengths. He completely satisfies the demands made by our desire for the candor he himself has led us to expect; yet he never compromises the desired image by reductive particularity.

If one hunts carefully through the *Life* one can find the mention of virtually every one of the unflattering descriptive details and peculiarities in one form or another. Yet as readers we experience them differently in the *Life* than we do in the other biographies of Johnson. Taken out of context, Boswell's two early descriptions of Johnson at table and the great man's oddities seem to contain many stark and vivid details. "His looks," says Boswell, "seemed rivetted to his plate; nor would he, unless when in very high company, say one word, or even pay the least attention to what was said by others, till he had satisfied his appetite, which was so fierce, and indulged with such intenseness, that while in the act of eating, the veins of his forehead swelled, and generally a strong perspiration was visible." Moreover,

> it is quite requisite to mention, that while talking or even musing
> as he sat in his chair, he commonly held his head to one side
> towards his right shoulder, and shook it in a tremulous manner,
> moving his body backwards and forwards, and rubbing his left

knee in the same direction, with the palm of his hand. In the intervals of articulating he made various sounds with his mouth, sometimes as if ruminating, or what is called chewing the cud, sometimes giving a half whistle, sometimes making his tongue play backwards from the roof of his mouth, as if clucking like a hen, and sometimes protruding it against his upper gums in front, as if pronouncing quickly under his breath, *too, too, too.*

Although these details are not quite so stark or unkind as most that are to be found in other biographies, it would be quibbling to cite small differences. As they stand these characteristics do not appear to be the stuff of which heroic images of the magnitude of Boswell's Johnson are made. But he never mentions them in this kind of detail again, and it is important to remember that the context from which these catalogues have been extracted is the *Life* as a whole—a large book in which we continuously imagine that we see Johnson as well as hear him.

Boswell does a number of things to counteract the potentially negative effect of Johnson's appearance and oddities; yet he has always succeeded in making us feel that we have seen Johnson—even at his worst. He does so by consistently invoking a single expressive (and almost always general) detail rather than resorting to a particular physical description. The bulk of the particulars are banked safely in the early portion of the book, and he draws on the balance extremely sparingly. I shall have more to say about this phenomenon below. One way to describe the result is to call it a literal version of metonymy in which reference to a part conjures up in our minds an image of the whole—but not a reductively specific image. It becomes the primary mode of perceiving Johnson throughout the majority of the *Life.* Who does not believe that he sees Johnson fully and clearly on the docks at Harwich as he sees Boswell off—Johnson "rolling his majestick frame in his usual manner"; or Johnson in a rage, "puffing hard with passion struggling for a vent"; or Johnson grappling with his fears of death, "standing upon the hearth rolling about with a serious, solemn, and somewhat gloomy air"; or Johnson in a lighter moment of banter with Miss Monckton, "smiling and rolling himself about"? These are the only concrete physically descriptive details in the respective scenes. The only other aids to our visualizing him are general, usually parenthetical, observations about his emotional state: "much agitated," "pointedly." The single word *rolling* in the above scenes conjures up, respectively, pictures of majesty, solemnity, powerful passion, and amused complacency. It is not, obviously, the word alone that does all this—it is the readers. We fill in the details; and we are guided always by Boswell's firm control (by other than descriptive means) of the image we will create. The "particulars" have been given to us early in the narrative, and we draw on them selectively. The tone, context, cues, and other direct statements by Boswell always set the stage, and one of the reasons that we visualize Johnson clearly is the same reason that we imagine we see changes of expression on the actually changeless face of a puppet. We make whatever details we see in our minds conform to the heroic image of Johnson to which our assent has cumulatively been gained. We see, in part, what we have been made to want to see. Perhaps the best and most delightful example of this is to be found in the famous Wilkes episode.

This episode must, by anybody's reckoning, rank among Boswell's finest performances. Everyone who has read it feels that Boswell had indeed kept his promise that we shall "live o'er each scene" with Johnson—see as well as hear him. Yet the descriptive touches that give the episode its imaginative and visual impact are remarkably minor. We actually see Johnson first in his library, "buffeting his books, as upon a former occasion, covered with dust." Aside from one other reference to Johnson's dustiness there are but two dramatic touches that conjure up a distinct physical image of him. The first is perhaps the most important to the episode: "When we entered Mr. Dilly's drawing room, he found himself in the midst of a company he did not know. I kept myself snug and silent, watching how he would conduct himself, I observed him whispering to Mr. Dilly, 'Who is that gentleman, Sir?'—'Mr. Arthur Lee.' JOHNSON 'Too, too, too,' (under his breath) which was one of his habitual mutterings."

Everything in the episode has been building to this moment. Johnson suddenly realizes (no doubt remembers now) where he is and what he has gotten into. He is temporarily disconcerted, hence "Too, too, too." The second crucial dramatic touch is a more elaborate physical description immediately following the revelation that the "gentleman in lace" is Mr. Wilkes, Sir." "This information" says Boswell, "confounded him still more; he had some difficulty to restrain himself, and taking up a book, sat down upon a window-seat and read, or at least kept his eye upon it intently for some time, till he composed himself." Without overparticularity (beads of perspiration or snorting) the image comically helps us gauge the extent of the impact. Boswell very rarely speculates openly about Johnson's state of mind. Will Johnson be able to make good his boast about not prescribing to a gentleman what company he is to have at his table? Will he bend the knee a little and yet maintain his dignity? Of course he does, as the delightful episode runs its course. If we are at all impregnated by the Johnsonian ether (simply from reading Boswell's book up to this point), we feel we are there at Dilly's. Boswell can be very particular when he wants to be: Wilkes says to Johnson, "Pray give me leave, Sir:—It is better here—A little of the brown—Some fat, Sir—a little of the stuffing." Johnson's famous reaction to Wilkes's assiduous attentions is a look of "surly virtue" (whatever that might mean in specific descriptive terms) but readers have always imagined that they have seen Johnson fully in both his discomfiture and his triumph. We feel that we see him more fully than one could reasonably predict on the basis of the amount of actual objective descriptive details. (There is no "protruding tongue" here, no "clucking like a hen.") We bring a cumulative and carefully controlled image of him with us to the episode. The slightest touch of the proper chord sets all the right vibrations stirring. We believe we see the rough edges of the great man; yet we actually see very little of a particular nature. He is made distinctive and unique without ever being made to seem grotesque or ungainly. Although we feel we have seen the warts, we are not invited to count the hairs on them.

Analogues of this same basic experience—we think we see one thing, but in fact we actually see another—exist for Boswell's treatment of almost every kind of apparently documentary, factual data. Until scholars had the perspective made possible by the discovery of Boswell's papers his artistry was virtually undetectable. It is doubly effective precisely because it successfully masquerades as total candor and strict adherence to the facts. A close comparison of the original journals (where they exist) or other primary sources and the final version they assume in the *Life* nearly always confirms this fact about the nature of Boswell's art in the *Life*. His shaping and controlling hand constantly alters the original, a coherent conception of Johnson's character informing the whole. But in the text of the *Life* he never compromises the impression that he is firmly tied to the facts whose faithful recorder he must always be; that it is they that control him, and not vice versa.

The account in the *Life* for July 14, 1763, is a good case in point. It occurs after the momentous first meeting, and the journal format has now become a part of the visual and psychological means of experiencing the Johnsonian record. The entry for July 14—the day on which Johnson first advises Boswell to keep a journal of his life—is a particularly full one. Such famous sparks are struck as that about Whiggism's being the negation of all principle; and, speaking of MacPherson's morals, Johnson thunders, "Sir, when he leaves our houses, let us count our spoons." It is a day momentous for Boswell and rich in Johnsonian matter. It is so because in fact it contains material from at least three or more days in the original journals, and because Boswell successfully practices all his accustomed wiles. He constantly "brushes up" Johnson's conversation in little ways: for example, "Why yes, Sir," for "Ay, Sir" in the original. He adds stage directions and slight descriptive touches: "feeling quite at ease," and so on. He puts words in Johnson's mouth that do not exist in the original and that in some instances are clearly added to make Johnson look better. "How much stronger are the evidences for the Christian religion," concludes Johnson in the *Life*, while in the original he had concluded by saying only, "Such is the weight of common testimony." Boswell even moves phrases about in Johnson's conversation. More than this, he adds a proportionately large amount of material that did not occur on the fourteenth at all—including the famous advice to keep a journal, which occurs in the original on the sixteenth. A long discussion about politics, including the famous remark about Whiggism, comes from another time, as does the reflection about counting spoons after a visit from MacPherson. He leaves out a wonderful vignette in the original in which Johnson judiciously prescribes the proper dosage of port wine for the evening. Presumably it was omitted because of the possible implications about Johnson's drinking—it appears in the manuscript of the first draft but is crossed out in pen and does not appear in the final version. In the famous advice about keeping a journal Boswell omits the fact (made clear in the original) that he was shocked at the idea of someone burning his journal after his death (Johnson's suggestion) and takes quite another view. Such changes, sweeping as some of them are, are certainly not surprising in the light of what we now know about Boswell's methods; but who would have questioned the published version of the *Life* if the Boswell papers did not exist? The impression created of Boswell's close tie to his primary factual documents is extremely convincing.

The impression of Boswell's general scrupulosity is made up of hundreds of separate instances of his reflections on it, his complaints of his inadequacy in this regard, his anguish over exactitude. Its potency is cumulative, its effect hypnotic, and its influence powerful indeed. The entry before that for the fourteenth is a single sentence (in the original manuscript of the *London Journal* it is simply a marginal note). "On Saturday, July 9, I found Johnson surrounded with a numerous levee, but have not preserved any part of his conversation." The original journals confirm this, but since it is so, why mention it at all? Its importance, I think, lies not in the information it retails, but in the impression it creates. He tells us everything—even that he recorded no conversation. He is scrupulously honest. Who would ever imagine that he would tell us *more* than he actually heard on a given day? All of the visual and formal documentary evidence encourage us not to ask such questions of the text. Boswell formally dates the entry for the fourteenth. He even describes the weather and dramatizes dialogues. We do "live o'er each scene" with Johnson here when Boswell writes, for example, "Why, Sir, (said he with a hearty laugh)." What grounds are there for suspecting that Boswell may be "shaping and controlling" here? The one thing that until recently has never been seriously questioned about the *Life* is its minute accuracy; but the powerful impression we get of it is often as much the result of Boswell's careful effort as it is the image of Johnson who is the book's subject.

The use of letters in the *Life* is particularly consistent with this technique of Boswell's. Letters make a strong visual and psychological impression (not just in epistolary novels), and Boswell depends heavily on them, especially in the early portion of the *Life*. He, of course, does theorize about their use in biography, and does "interweave what [Johnson] privately wrote, said, and thought." Yet it is now a known fact that he omitted letters that he felt to be inappropriate to the image of Johnson that he built; that he sometimes altered their contents; and that many times he achieved the same results with them in the text of the *Life* that he did with details of Johnson's appearance and oddities. Our response to the image of Johnson that the *Life* projects is conditioned by similar controls, and one of Boswell's greatest successes in this regard is his use of what many have argued are vast amounts of raw data, such as Boswell's law cases, that have little or no apparent connection with Johnson. Looked at closely, our experience of these data is not a problem but a desired effect. Here, as elsewhere, Boswell makes a potential liability into a powerful literary asset.

The book begins technically not with the well-known "To write the life of him, . . ." but with a chronological catalogue of Johnson's known works, a catalogue that Greene shrewdly suggests Boswell could have been more scrupulous about even at the time. We experience the flow of data visually as well as intellectually—names, law cases, degrees with the Latin text accompanying them and signed. For example:

Anno Domini millesimo septigentisimo-quinto.

'Gul. Clement.	Fran. Andrews.	R. Murray
'Tho. Wilson	Praeps.	Cus.
'Tho. Leland.		Rob. Law.
		Mich. Kearney.

Boswell even includes such things as an anecdote about a woman who fell hopelessly in love with Michael Johnson and apparently died of love for him. The full episode is related and the inscription on her grave is included in the *Life*. "Here lies the body of Mrs. Elizabeth Blaney, a stranger. She departed the life 20 of September, 1694."

One response to the inclusion of such material—and there is indeed a multitude of it—has always been to suggest that it is unassimilable and therefore a limitation, however great the work. Another is to suggest that such data are doing their job simply by being data, ratifying, by their very presence, the major premise on which the success of Boswell's book rests and that is the major precondition of his art.

In the *Life* Boswell is more concerned with truth than he is with facts per se, and the distinction is an extremely important one. He formally states many times that his subject is Johnson's *character*, and this as an artistic principle of the *Life* has been confirmed repeatedly by modern scholars. As in the case with most complex human beings, the most important "truths" about Johnson's character were not empirically verifiable. Interpretations had to be made, gaps filled imaginatively, and meanings conferred on previously meaningless factual data. Boswell was, moreover, making much more than the faithful record of a man—he was creating Schwartz's historical personage with some of the trappings of a fictional character. Yet, I shall argue that in the *Life* the success of the literary effects depends directly on the credibility of the image of the historical man. Boswell anchors his image of Johnson so firmly in concrete facts and explicit details that he confers on his interpretive portrait the impact of absolute historical truth. John Wilson Croker's famous error and Donald Stauffer's enthusiasm about Boswell's facts are, I think, more understandable when considered in this light. They are quite believable responses to effects that Boswell was trying very hard to create.

In fiction the effect created by Boswell's mountains of data has a clear and common analogue that is normally called verisimilitude. We are used to thinking of the marvels of the world of Defoe, or the imaginative extravagances of Dickens anchored firmly to weights, sizes, shapes, and particular streets and places. The concept of verisimilitude usually implies that something other than the truth is being disguised by its aid, but the recipient of the aid need not always be an untruth; and the concept need not be considered applicable to fiction alone. It can give power to interpretive statement and legitimate biographical speculation as well; and it does so in the *Life*.

Boswell's treatment of Johnson's death is especially instructive in this regard. There was much interest in how the great moralist would die, and there are probably more extended accounts of this one incident than of any other in Johnson's life. Unlike many who wrote on the subject, Boswell was not present. Moreover, by the time he wrote the *Life* he was, we know now, in possession of evidence that he felt was potentially contradictory to the image of his great moral symbol. He had incontrovertible evidence that Johnson had thought of remarriage and that his mind clung to memories of his wife and marriage for perhaps other than the most pleasing reasons. He apparently knew even more specifically some of the "sins" connected with Johnson's conduct toward his wife, some of the things that gave him the greatest uneasiness. Boswell's extended account of Johnson's last year and of his death is perhaps his most sophisticated and sustained performance.

He builds from the beginning of the final year: "And now I am arrived at the last year of the life of Samuel Johnson." He begins systematically to place every incident in the context of coming events: the last time at the Literary Club; the last time Boswell is under his roof; the last Johnsonian utterances. He becomes more and more exasperated at his inadequacies in perserving the Johnsonian record—"When I now look back to it, I am vexed that a single word should have been forgotten." (It is the kind of admission of weakness that actually implies great strength.) There is the final leave-taking of the two from which Johnson springs away without looking back, "with a kind of pathetic briskness." And then factual data begin to multiply along with reflections on the great man: an attack on Mrs. Thrale, a testimony to Johnson's love for Tetty, then letters and more letters, and large and larger footnotes, swelling the tide of undeniable actuality and total disclosure. (Boswell admits freely that he was not present at Johnson's last days; yet the degree to which he is successful in making us feel that we are is remarkable.) All the difficult moral questions seem to be confronted directly. Boswell himself brings up Johnson's fears of death. He admits reluctantly but gravely—in the interest of complete candor—that Johnson was guilty of indiscretions whose weight he presumably now felt. "In short, it must not be concealed, that, like many other good and pious men, among whom we may place the Apostle Paul upon his own authority, Johnson was not free from propensities which were ever 'warring against the law of his mind'—and that in his combats with them, he was sometimes overcome." Boswell assures us that it was not foolish scrupulosity on Johnson's part— not "venial trifles as pouring milk into his tea on Good Friday"—that troubled Johnson. Great men have great passions and great struggles with them; but if Johnson's *practice* was occasionally faulty, his principles were steadfast and his honesty with himself was, as always, ruthless. Who among us, asks Boswell, is pure enough to cast the first stone at Johnson? Boswell concludes the section formally:

> I am conscious that this is the most difficult and dangerous part of my biographical work, and I cannot but be very anxious concerning it. I trust that I have got through it, preserving at once my regard to truth,—to my friend,—and to the interests of virtue and religion. Nor can I apprehend that more harm can ensue from the knowledge of the irregularity of Johnson, guarded as I have stated it, than from knowing that Addison and Parnell were intemperate in the use of wine.

Boswell makes it clear that he has taken a great risk. He is baring Johnson's soul; he is apparently telling everything—no matter what the risk. Who, unless in retrospect and in the light of concrete evidence to the contrary, can believe that he has held anything back? The illusion is very powerful. But almost everything is not everything; generalities are not specifics, and recent discoveries make it clear that he was holding something back and must have known that he was.

An interpretive biographer whose dramatic choices were his interpretive statements, Boswell knew when and when not to tell everything. Hawkins in his record of Johnson's death builds to an account of the results of an autopsy on Johnson. "The report was to this effect: Two of the valves of the aorta ossified. The air cells of the lungs usually distended. One of the kidneys destroyed by the pressure of the water. The liver schirrhous. A stone in the bladder the size of a common gooseberry." Boswell omits these undeniable facts and leads instead to the famous remarks of Hamilton: "He has made a chasm, which not only nothing can fill up, but which nothing has a tendency to fill up.—Johnson is dead.—Let us go to the next best:—there is nobody;—no man can be said to put you in mind of Johnson."

In biography the opposite of fact is not always fiction, and the opposite of historical truth is not necessarily a lie. As Marshall Waingrow observes when musing on the patterns of Boswell's suppressions in the *Life*,

> his indolence, his oddities and asperity of manner, his excesses in eating and drinking, his profanity and bawdy, his sexual lapses, his intellectual narrowness and prejudice, his use of drugs, his insanity—all of these subjects appear among the unused sources, and all seem to compose themselves into a pattern of suppression.

Yet it is an equally demonstrable fact that all of these subjects are admitted to the published work in one form or another. Whatever construction Boswell may have put upon Johnson's weakness, it cannot be said that he concealed either the fact or the issue.

The key words in the above remarks are, I believe, those that suggest that virtually everything is admitted to the published work "in one form or another." It is clearly the form their admittance takes that determines our reaction to them; and I believe Waingrow's feelings accurately describe not the causes but the effects of Boswell's methods. Except for the two known instances of suppression of fact noted above, it would be difficult to demonstrate that Boswell seriously exceeds the proper bounds of the interpretive or speculative biographer. The problem is that he claims that he is neither when in fact he is both. The questions then become, Is this honest biography? Is this kind of relation between the facts, the art, and the biographical intent permissible?

James Boswell: Theory and Practice of Biography

Frank Brady

Boswell's *Life of Johnson*, "the delight and boast of the English-speaking world," is by common consent the greatest biography ever written. Beyond that judgement, disagreement about its nature and characteristics is so various and deep that this chapter must restrict itself to five issues: (1) biographical theory and practice as they are related to the *Life*; (2) the making of the *Life*; (3) its presentation of Johnson; (4) Boswell as author and character; (5) eighteenth-century and modern critical opinion of the *Life*.

A satisfactory theory of biography depends on the assumption that a biography is a work of fact and not fiction. Fact and fiction evoke fundamentally different mental sets, and faced with a written work a reader is profoundly uneasy until he knows which set is appropriate. Tell a six-year-old a story, and the first question he will ask is whether it is real or pretend. For adults, the question of whether the Bible is a work of fact or of fiction, even if fiction of the greatest significance, arouses argument so passionate that until a few centuries ago it could cost a man his life, and can still cost him his job. Authenticity, Boswell's proudest claim for the *Life* as for his other biographical works, meant above all to him truth to fact.

The differences in response to fiction and fact are far easier to suggest than to define. Fiction widens into potentiality, while fact offers the pleasing resistance of the actual. Fiction may move us more deeply, but we trust fact. Fictional characters can be developed to any degree of complexity, but who

From *James Boswell: The Later Years, 1769-1795*. Copyright © 1984 by Frank Brady. McGraw-Hill Book Co., 1984. Originally entitled "The Life."

can say where the resonance of real persons like Garrick and Burke dies out? Fictional narrative can please with wonderful invention, but factual narrative invites increased alertness: if this happened to someone else, it could happen to me.

The mental set of fiction derives from imagination, and of fact from memory. Of course the two must overlap: imagination becomes unintelligible if it loses touch with what we already know, while memory involves imaginative reconstruction. But there are essential distinctions between "imaginative" modes, like drama or the novel, and "memorial" modes, like biography and history.

Imaginative works are closed forms, while memorial works are open ones. *Don Quixote* is a self-limiting novel; nothing more can be learned about its hero because he was not a real person. But the *Life of Johnson* is permeable, so to speak; the adequacy of its Johnson can be checked by information from other sources, just as we impart to Boswell's depiction certain characteristics drawn from other works about him. A character in a novel has only to be plausible, but the subject of a biography must be credible. At most, novels can be compared; biographies can be corrected. Usually a biography is too full of the unresolved dissonances typical of our own lives to attain the satisfying conclusion of a novel.

The eighteenth century thought much more highly of factual literature than of fiction; today the opposite is true. This shift in prestige to the imagined or imaginatively reconstituted is partly responsible for obscuring the biographical traditions on which Boswell drew. Virtually all serious biography before Boswell's time was ethical; its model in purpose was Plutarch's *Lives,* and its aim to instruct and to judge. This noble tradition now seems pompous because of our distaste for the explicitly didactic, but Johnson justifies it when he asserts, "We are perpetually moralists, but we are geometricians only by chance." Johnson is not suggesting that we adopt a high moral tone or spy on our neighbours. He is merely emphasizing that the most important decisions we make every day are ethical decisions. Basically, we are ethical beings; our intellectual knowledge of the world is, by comparison, unimportant. And biography has the advantage over history, its rival among memorial genres, of offering individual rather than general models of thought and behaviour. "I esteem biography," Johnson told Lord Monboddo, "as giving us what comes near to ourselves, what we can turn to use."

But the kernel and origin of biography is the anecdote, nothing more than the story one person tells to a second about a third; and the tradition of anecdotal biography is also long, going back at least to Xenophon's *Memorabilia* of Socrates. One basic distinction between the two types is that in ethical biography incident serves the humble function of illustrating moral points, while in anecdotal biography incident comes to the fore and the ethical is apt to be left to fend for itself. In the eighteenth century, though anecdotal biography had strong admirers, including Johnson himself, it was open to the charge that it pandered to idle curiosity—a frequent criticism, as mentioned, of the *Hebrides*—and lacked redeeming moral value.

Johnson's two important pre-Boswellian biographers neatly illustrate the extremes of ethical and anecdotal types. Hawkins's *Life of Johnson* plucks out the moral *exempla* to be derived from Johnson's career, but Johnson himself peers through only at intervals. In contrast, his character—often in its most unpleasant moods—emerges vividly in the brief, disjointed stories that make up Mrs. Piozzi's *Anecdotes*, which is a classic of moral confusion.

Boswell made the necessary connection: his *Life of Johnson* embodies a crucial moment in the history of biography because in it he unifies the ethical and anecdotal traditions. (In the same period, Gibbon similarly unified the traditions of philosophical and antiquarian history.) And Boswell extended a third biographical element, the role of psychological analysis. For this he had Johnson's example in the *Lives of the Poets* to go on. But he also had his own journal-practice as background, as well as models of introspection ranging from confessions and autobiographies by splendid saints and sinners, like Augustine and Rousseau, to those of spiritual and temporal journalists whom a contemporary unkindly referred to as "a thousand . . . old women and fanatic writers."

General tradition and concrete example operate in any particular biography through its major determinants: materials, methods of presentation, and, most important, purpose. And purpose in the biography of a writer also has shifted over the years. In the recent past, the usefulness of a "critical biography," one that purports to connect life and work, was thought to consist mainly in giving the work a limiting context. Although biography, in this approach, cannot fix intention in the old-fashioned sense of "Milton wanted to show in *Lycidas* that . . ." it can establish, while making more precise, a possible range of meanings. A knowledge of Boswell's life and character, for example, rules out the notion, which has actually been advanced, that the *Life of Johnson* is basically a covert attack on its subject.

But this is a minimal view of the function of critical biography, and reflects the clichés of formal criticism, the most anti-biographical of theories, rather than even its usual practice. Intent on preserving the isolated purity of the literary work, its good-for-nothingness except as a locus of aesthetic and moral values, the formal critic ostensibly restricted his analysis to the thing-in-itself, while constantly drawing—though without notice—on what in rigorous theory was inadmissible evidence, starting with his knowledge of the writer's career and era.

Today, when the range of critical approaches has widened beyond the narrow verities of formal criticism, we are permitted an ampler view of critical biography. To understand any literary work requires, to begin with, a grasp of its genre and of its historical context. Equally essential is a personal context—of which Boswell's is a model at its fullest—that biography provides to put the subject's work in adequate perspective. The work never provides sufficient information in itself for proper interpretation. To fully grasp Johnson's *Lives of the Poets*, for instance, it helps to know something about the circumstances in which Johnson wrote it, his own feelings about his subjects, and his personality and prejudices.

A modern biographer might focus on his subject's writings, but in Boswell's approach Johnson's writings took their place in a more inclusive vision of Johnson as a struggling moral hero of everyday life—a hero and a life to be presented on an epic scale. In the Advertisement to the second edition, Boswell points to his epic model when he compares the *Life* to the *Odyssey*, in that "amidst a thousand entertaining and instructive episodes the HERO is never long out of sight, for they are all in some degree connected with him; and HE in the whole course of the history is exhibited by the author for the best advantage of his readers." Boswell then quotes two lines from Horace (given here in Francis's translation):

> To show what wisdom and what sense can do
> The poet sets Ulysses in our view.

Nor is it surprising that Boswell thought of a moral struggle in epic terms: what else is *Paradise Lost*, which has hung over all later English epics? The *Life of Johnson* takes its place among the many eighteenth-century versions of epic: Pope's translation of the *Iliad, Rape of the Lock*, and *Dunciad; Tom Jones; The Decline and Fall of the Roman Empire*; and those strangest of mutations, Blake's major prophecies. When the epic returns in changed but recognizable form, its hero, the narrator of Wordsworth's *Prelude*, is like Johnson an ordinary man who has taken on some of the aura of the sublime.

Within the epic framework, Boswell wanted to present his hero both fully and exactly. Fullness, given his materials, was a comparatively easy achievement. "I will venture to say," he writes at the beginning of the *Life*, that Johnson "will be seen in this work more completely than any man who has ever yet lived." Full presentation of a hero aligns Boswell with the ethical tradition.

Exactness, on the other hand, might seem an impossible ideal. As Geoffrey Scott says: "Boswell has an image which describes his aim: a 'life' should be like a flawless print struck off from the engraved plate which is bitten in our memory. . . . Biography should be nothing less than this duplication of an image in the mind." Or, to cite Boswell directly, "I must be exact as to every line in his countenance, every hair, every mole." If this was beyond anyone's power he could at least create, in his celebrated phrase, a "Flemish picture" of Johnson that expanded anecdotal biography beyond any earlier conception.

The sheer quantity of Boswell's material, beginning with his massive journal, put fullness and exactness within reach. But quantity also helped to force a new biographical approach on him. In his "Memoirs of Pascal Paoli," where his notes were somewhat sparse and he wanted to disguise the fact that his visit to Paoli had lasted only a week, Boswell suppressed dates and filled out his account by interspersing what Paoli said and did with general comment on the Corsicans. A contrasting problem emerged in the *Hebrides*, where he worried that his narrative would be choked with detail; there he experimented by abridging it under topographical headings (St. Andrews, Laurencekirk), until he reverted with great success to the day-by-day entries of his original journal.

But the method that served for a three-month narrative like the *Hebrides* would not do for a far more comprehensive portrait and, as early as 1780, Boswell had determined to write the *Life of Johnson* "in scenes," that is, to centre his presentation on conversations which would approximate scenes in a play. This was a key decision and it meant that Johnson, whom Boswell praises in the opening sentence of the *Life* as the greatest of biographers, could not provide an appropriate model. Though Johnson included dialogue and anecdote, the principal interest of his *Lives of the Poets* lay in his unrelenting judgemental commentary. This suited neither Boswell's aim nor his material.

Instead, early in the *Life* Boswell announces, "I have resolved to adopt and enlarge upon the excellent plan of Mr. Mason, in his *Memoirs of [Thomas] Gray.*" Well known at the time, William Mason's *Gray* was unusual in being made up of a long series of the subject's letters—which Mason, we now know, rephrased, bowdlerized, truncated, spliced together, and misdated—linked by a trickle of mealy-mouthed explanation. But even in these butchered versions Gray's letters, as Boswell remarked to Temple, "show us the *man.*" They present Gray so directly, they reveal so much about him, that Mason the memoirist is forgotten and Gray stands before us plain. Self-presentation and self-revelation by his subject to the greatest extent possible: this too was part of Boswell's plan. Of course he had been born knowing how to set figures directly before an audience, as he had shown in his earlier studies of Paoli and Johnson. But Mason's example may have crystallized his decision about how to present Johnson in the *Life,* and at the least it offered a convenient precedent.

To the union of the ethical and anecdotal on an epic scale, Boswell joined, then, one more innovation of the greatest significance to biography: mimesis, the setting of a subject immediately before the reader. "Presentness" was the decisive effect Boswell wanted to achieve: to get Johnson to present himself, to reveal himself, first in conversation, but also in all those documents Boswell quotes or summarizes: letters, prayers and meditations, essays and biographies with working notes and discarded readings, political pamphlets, definitions, parodies, fables and allegories, decisions on literary disputes, an appeal for votes, poems, legal opinions, a novel, and even the minor forms of eulogy—dedication, obituary, and epitaph. Johnson appears further in what was said about him in various forms, from diplomas to memorable opinions: Garrick's "Johnson gives you a forcible hug and shakes laughter out of you, whether you will or no"; Goldsmith's "he has nothing of the bear but his skin"; Dr. John Boswell's "a robust genius born to grapple with whole libraries." Presentness is the brightest of Boswell's talents. He became the first mimetic biographer and he remains without equal.

II

If the glory of art is to conceal art, then the *Life of Johnson* belongs in the first rank. Finally the naive notion has passed that Boswell practised a primitive stenography, so that he had no more to do than to copy out his tablets, but its long persistence testifies to Boswell's success: it was the effect on which all other effects depended. The making of the *Life* had to be a much more complicated task.

Boswell's rawest material was the condensed notes which he made as soon as possible after the event recorded, sometimes on the same day. When he had expanded these, presumably they were to be disposed of, though a good many survive besides those which he never wrote up. Sometimes as late as the *Life* itself he would expand a brief jotting into a whole speech or scene. So the note, "Johns[on] great on Lit[erary] Prop[er]ty. Creation for autho[r]. But consent of nations ag[ainst]," became a Johnsonian utterance 170 words long.

But the journal was the prime source for most of the scenes displayed in the *Life*, with torn-out leaves used directly as copy. As in revising for the *Hebrides*, Boswell dramatized as much as possible; indirect discourse was recast as dialogue and, in playing back scenes in his mind, vivifying detail, sometimes in the form of stage directions, might materialize in so advanced a stage as proofs. These directions could be as brief as "smiling," or expand to "standing upon the hearth rolling about, with a serious, solemn, and somewhat gloomy air." But in every case they fix an expression or gesture or tone of voice.

We know that Boswell's reports of conversations could not be verbatim. But as early as 1762, Boswell wrote of an hour-and-a-half session with David Hume, which he preserved in a 900-word précis: "I have remembered the heads and the very words of a great part of Mr. Hume's conversation"; and this much he could claim. What the *Life* provides is a selection or epitome of Johnson's talk. Once well acquainted with his phrasing and syntax— "*strongly impregnated with the Johnsonian ether*"—Boswell could surround pivotal words with characteristic diction. (In a contest of Johnsonian mimicry, the umpire Hannah More adjudged superiority to Garrick in reading poetry and to Boswell in familiar conversation, a convincing testimonial to his ability to catch Johnson's voice, phrasing, and manner.) If Johnson didn't say precisely what Boswell records him as saying, he said something very much like it.

But how accurate is this presentation? In the Advertisement to the first edition, an essay in self-praise, Boswell called attention to the work the *Life* had necessitated:

> The labour and anxious attention with which I have collected
> and arranged the materials of which these volumes are composed
> will hardly be conceived by those who read them with careless
> facility. The stretch of mind and prompt assiduity by which so
> many conversations were preserved, I myself, at some distance
> of time, contemplate with wonder; and I must be allowed to
> suggest that the nature of the work in other respects, as it consists
> of innumerable detached particulars, all which, even the most

minute, I have spared no pains to ascertain with a scrupulous authenticity, has occasioned a degree of trouble far beyond that of any other species of composition.

Boswell's final claim is excessive, but his feeling is understandable. He had first to deal with that "great sand-drift of 'particulars' he had accumulated since 1763," while he collected and sifted the contributions of others. Since authenticity is the scaffolding of the *Life*, he was careful, for the most part, to cite his authorities wherever it counted, constantly reassuring his reader that the narrative is solidly based, yet at the same time leaving to him some of the responsibility for assessing the evidence.

Attention to truth was a distinguishing feature of the Johnsonian school, but even before Boswell met Johnson his father had beaten the same principle into him. He was continually on guard. "Carelessness as to the exactness of circumstances is very dangerous," he said, "for one may gradually recede from the fact till all is fiction." In writing, "one must clear head (lave it [ladle it out] as a boat of water) of imagination to give authentic narration." When Boswell came to a disputed point, such as who was responsible for Johnson's pension, he cross-examined every witness, a procedure Johnson had taught him to extend from the courtroom into daily life:

> *Lord Bute told me* that Mr. Wedderburn, now Lord Loughborough, was the person who first mentioned this subject to him. *Lord Loughborough told me* that the pension was granted to Johnson solely as the reward of his literary merit. . . . *Mr. Thomas Sheridan and Mr. Murphy*, who then lived a good deal both with him and Mr. Wedderburn, *told me* that they previously talked with Johnson upon this matter. . . . *Sir Joshua Reynolds told me* that Johnson called on him.

In preparing the *Life* for publication, the only sustained help Boswell received was from Malone, and the precise extent of that help will not be clear until the manuscript is fully deciphered and edited. But already it is evident that Malone's share, though substantial, was less than it had been in the case of the *Hebrides*. Malone got Boswell started on the *Life* and kept him at it. When Boswell had completed most of the draft he read it aloud to Malone, who made suggestions; then they worked together through about half the proofs—this book, like the *Hebrides*, was being printed off as they concluded revision— before Malone's departure for Ireland. Malone had taught Boswell how to go over a manuscript with diligence, and continued to offer advice from across the Irish Sea: "Pray take care of colloquialisms and vulgarisms of all sorts. Condense as much as possible, always preserving perspicuity, and do not imagine the *only* defect of style is repetition of words." Boswell replied sadly that the difference between what they had revised together and what he had done by himself was only too visible, but it has never been apparent to readers.

Pursuit of accuracy entailed no unthinking reverence for documents, and the process of reworking that Boswell applied to his own Johnsoniana he applied even more vigorously to the accounts contributed by others, subjecting them "to every conceivable mode of revision: summary, paraphrase, expansion, conflation, interpolation, and so forth." A modern editor of the "His Very Self and Voice" persuasion would have left them as they were, but such compilations are material for a biography, not its substitute. Biography cannot consist of bits and pieces, the unmediated clamour of conflicting views. Documents must be fused within a smooth, coherent narrative. Authenticity depends on accuracy as the basis for the biographer's image of his subject. Still, "*perfect* authenticity," as Marshall Waingrow remarks, "is to be found not in the discrete historical fact, but in its representation—in the control of implications."

Method of presentation, however, does depend in the *Life of Johnson* on the discrete fact, and Boswell was much more confident than he had been in writing the *Hebrides* that particulars were vital, with the selection and arrangement of these particulars regulated by "a massively detailed conception of Johnson's character, operating to shape into unity all the multifarious and potentially discordant elements of a very long book." Boswell necessarily builds his world out of facts, but facts as construed by a powerful and wide-ranging sense of actuality, comparable to what we call imagination in a novelist.

Does this mean, as G. B. Shaw asserted, that Boswell was the dramatist who invented Johnson? Shaw is right to the extent that all biographers invent their subjects; just as we speak of Lockhart's Scott and Strachey's Victoria, so this is Boswell's Johnson. Boswell's aim was authenticity, not "objectivity." There never was nor ever can be an "objective" Johnson; even Johnson's own view of himself, though privileged, is only one view among others.

III

In his presentation of Johnson, Boswell was able to fit material to purpose smoothly. The first fifth of the *Life*, which describes Johnson's career until their meeting in 1763, serves to introduce the detailed portrait of the mature man. The structure of the main section, a potentially difficult problem, was handled very simply. Johnson's life in his middle and late years lacked eventfulness or even much incident: except for excursions to Scotland, Wales, and France in successive years, each year saw him follow a familiar round. So Boswell emphasized continuity by dividing his material chronologically, year by year, without chapter breaks. This mechanical organization provides just enough dividing lines to give the material a shape without impeding its flow: the movement through scene, summary, commentary, and quotation that builds up the *Life*'s alternation between drama and documentary. At the same time, chronological organization satisfied Boswell's desire that the reader " 'live o'er each scene,' " with Johnson, "as he actually advanced through the several stages of his life."

Lacking narrative urgency, the *Life* at its basic level of appeal is picked up with anticipation, put down with equanimity, and returned to with pleasure. "The book of Boswell is ever, as the year comes round, my winter's-evening's entertainment," wrote Richard Cumberland. Sir Walter Scott thought it "the best parlour-window book that ever was written." George Mallory caught some sense of the *Life*'s engagingness in a simple impressionistic comment: "The plain fact is that it is impossible to read Boswell without feeling better. . . . With Boswell we never want to leave the world for something better, but we want to live in it and enjoy life to the full; and we want especially to love other men."

The *Life* does keep calling the reader back. Boswell compensates for the lack of sustained development or intriguing suspense with local effects: the constant shift from conversation to reflection to letter; and the use of multiple perspectives: Johnson as he sees himself, past and present, in reminiscence and diary entry; Johnson as Boswell sees him; and, in unusual diversity, Johnson as other contemporaries see him. We keep coming back to Johnson from different angles. Individual scenes, the most famous being the Johnson-Wilkes meeting at the Dillys' dinner in 1776, combine surprise, recognition, reversal—all the techniques dramatists use; but these effects always return us to the centre of interest, the life and opinions, the progressions and digressions, of Johnson himself. His "exuberant variety of . . . wisdom and wit," operating within a framework of predictable attitudes but always forceful and unexpected in expression, focuses and holds the reader's attention.

At the same time, Boswell stresses the stability of repetition. The unity of the *Life* is largely thematic: the same topics, though raised from shifting points of view, appear again and again. Also, the cast of characters changes with reluctance; even the same actions recur:

BOSWELL.   "Let us dine by ourselves at the Mitre, to keep up the old custom, 'the custom of the manor,' the custom of the Mitre."
JOHNSON.   "Sir, so it shall be."

Time, too, repeats itself. After 1763, except for two autumnal interludes, it is always spring in the *Life*. The years themselves pass in the steady march of days. How familiar and comforting to the habitual reader of the *Life* are its temporal cadences: "on Monday, April 6," "on Thursday, April 9," "on Friday, April 10," "on Saturday, April 11." These markers lack any individual distinctiveness or importance; it is only the sequence that counts, as it insists on dailiness, on the way we all experience life, just day by day.

Setting is equally generalized and unemphatic. Sometimes a few props; but usually Boswell does no more than indicate place, and continues: "There was a pretty large circle this evening. Dr. Johnson was in very good humour, lively, and ready to talk upon all subjects." The details are precisely sufficient to let us know where we are; they provide solidity without specification.

The character of Johnson, at the centre of the *Life*, also is static. The modern biographer tends to conceive of his subject in terms of development; but Boswell, like his contemporaries, believed that the boy is the man in miniature, and thought instead of persistent, lifelong traits. Johnson of course had a career: he attended Oxford, progressed from failed schoolmaster to London author by profession, became the dominant literary figure of his time: in turn poet, biographer, lexicographer, essayist, novelist, editor, and critic. But from the beginning his innate intellectual superiority, his "astonishing force and vivacity of mind," his "supereminent powers" displayed themselves. And other characteristics were equally prominent: "jealous independence of spirit and impetuosity of temper," "dismal inertness of disposition," and "morbid melancholy." Activated by his conviction of free will and deep Christian belief, Johnson struggled to reform, and was caught, according to one Boswellian formulation, in the "vibration between pious resolutions and indolence." Boswell insists sympathetically on this striving, on both accomplishment and failure. But the bases of character do not change.

Though character was static, the eighteenth century gave it range by insisting that it was composed of contradictions, and Johnson's contradictions were emphatic; he was all the more difficult to portray, as Steevens pointed out, because "his particularities and frailties" were more strongly marked than his virtues. Boswell was intent on depicting him as "blinking Sam" and all, but his faults had to be put in perspective; this meant that Boswell had to counteract the common misconception that Johnson was a gloomy, brutal pedant, while avoiding the opposite extreme of the hero as grand old character.

A contemporary biographer might have taken refuge in a "ruling passion," just as a modern biographer might reduce Johnson to fit the pattern of what very loosely may be called "the authoritarian personality": guilty, domineering, perfectionistic, rigid in religion and politics, self-disapproving and harsh towards others—a giant in chains. Insecurities within emerged as hard-edged formulations: "The woman's a whore, and there's an end on't." But equally Johnson was honest, warm-hearted, helpful, and hugely affectionate. A biographer could impale himself on these contradictions, as Mrs. Piozzi had; her Johnson was not only repulsive, he was unbelievable to those who had known him.

Boswell solved this problem of presentation brilliantly. In the *Hebrides*, he had begun with a block sketch of Johnson. Now far more confident of his method and material, Boswell could rely on an accumulation of minute particulars to build up "a full, fair, and distinct view" of Johnson's character: it is an *emergent* picture that makes the reader acquainted with Johnson in the same way he comes, little by little, to know a friend.

In amassing particulars, Boswell takes full advantage of his claim to "authentic precision." Since it predisposes the reader to believe in his truthfulness, Boswell does not need to worry about plausibility. A fictional character is judged on the basis of congruence: does the reader, relying on experience, find his traits coherent? But a real person puts the burden of explanation on the observer: what patterns make sense of his actions? And Boswell had piled up, from his own records and those of others, a collection of examples that showed an unusually complex range of acts and characteristics. He exhibited not only the well-known Johnson, decisive in opinion and abrupt in response, but a Johnson who was tender and warm in feeling; who had a sense of humour—grave, robust, or sly—"which gives an oiliness and a gloss to every other quality"; who even exhibited a "politeness and urbanity" for which he did not often get credit. At the same time, Boswell can put unpleasant incidents into perspective with explanation—"the fretfulness of his disease unexpectedly showed itself"—or examples of Johnson's deep sympathy and ready practical assistance. As Waingrow says, Boswell presents Johnson's weaknesses under aspects of his strengths.

We learn so much about this Johnson because there is so much to learn.

Sometimes Boswell points up opposites: the slovenly body contrasted with the acute mind; the contractions, tics, and mutters with the strength, precision, and aptness of expression. Taken as a whole, Johnson gradually grows in impressiveness: he demonstrates "wit" (defined by James Thomson as "vivid energy of sense") and "wisdom" (the same common sense concentrated to high generality). Wit and wisdom combine in his power to penetrate to the core of ordinary experience. In Percy's phrase, he "at once probed the human heart, where the sore was."

And so, gradually, Boswell not merely asserts but establishes a dominant image of this "great and good man," of Johnson's generous humanity, which then allows him to concede almost any number of limitations and failings without essentially depreciating Johnson's character. Though the *Life* was written in "admiration and reverence" (its last words), for Boswell warm partisanship was compatible with shrewd observation and, at moments, detached amusement. Boswell sees all round Johnson. He is not only a hero but an extraordinary specimen of human character. The great philosopher can scold the waiter about roast mutton: "It is as bad as bad can be. It is ill-fed, ill-killed, ill-kept, and ill-dressed." He can be shown as overbearing, narrow-minded, susceptible to flattery, greedy for victory, superstitious, and self-deceived. Most dangerous, Boswell can make him look comic:

> If we may believe Mr. Garrick, his old master's taste in theatrical merit was by no means refined; he was not an *elegans formarum spectator* ["a nice observer of the female form" (Terence, *Eunuch*, iii.5)]. Garrick used to tell that Johnson said of an actor who played Sir Harry Wildair at Lichfield: "There is a courtly vivacity about the fellow"; when in fact, according to Garrick's account, "He was the most vulgar ruffian that ever went upon *boards*."

But Johnson's shortcomings humanize him, and even his small acts become attractive. Boswell writes:

> He sent for me to his bedside and expressed his satisfaction at this incidental meeting with as much vivacity as if he had been in the gaiety of youth. He called briskly, "Frank, go and get coffee, and let us breakfast *in splendour*."

Boswell's insistence on full credibility allows him to move from detail to generalization and back again with ease. We believe that Johnson showed an "eager and unceasing curiosity to know human life in all its variety," in part because of the scenes already exhibited, and in part simply because

Boswell says so. Johnson's character takes on a density that makes other fine biographical portraits, such as the acute and elegant profiles of Strachey, seem as impoverished as the ordinary fictional figure. No one ever travelled all over this man's mind. In Boswell's depiction, Johnson attains a "critical mass," like Don Quixote or Hamlet; he becomes capable, within the broad limits of his beliefs and prejudices, of saying or doing anything and, indeed, his unpredictability becomes a compelling attribute. Readers agree with John Nichols that "every fragment of so great a man is worthy of being preserved"; even the most trivial detail—that he tried to pole a large dead cat along a stream—makes him that much more visible. And when these details are amassed, Johnson's significance overflows any single interpretation, and causes each age to construe him differently. His contemporaries, to simplify, beheld the great lexicographer, moralist, and critic; for the nineteenth century he became the epitome of strong uncommon sense; and some modern commentators suggest an anguished figure sustained by force of will from moment to moment over the void.

Boswell's portrayal, however, does not focus on an isolated Johnson; like most eighteenth-century writers, he thinks of the individual first as a social being. Johnson must have a human context. And so the importance of Boswell's large treasure of Johnsonian conversation. It was the "peculiar value" of the *Life,* whose main business, Boswell said, was to record it. But it was also the central activity of the *Life* in all its settings: tête-à-têtes, small casual gatherings, formal dinners, meetings of The Club. Here are the great scenes that make Johnson's *dramatic* portrait, the single most distinctive and most often discussed aspect of the *Life.*

Though from time to time Boswell collects what he calls "gold dust" (detached remarks), Johnson's sayings carry more weight when they emerge in such social contexts, often under the pressure of informal argument. Johnson believed conversation was a high art where a man's intellectual ability truly proved itself, while public speaking was merely a knack. Conversation for him naturally turned into contest, and Johnson was formidable: he could speak on any subject with fluency and impact; his adroitness of response was notorious; his talk "teemed with point and imagery"; and if all else failed he knocked down his opponent with sophistry or sarcasm. Again and again Boswell illustrates its "unexampled richness and brilliancy," which only Burke among contemporaries could rival. In talking, Johnson is brought close up: we are in the same room with him; he sits directly in front of us and we see the expression on his face; he speaks to us; we hear him laugh and growl; we could almost reach out and touch him.

The great web of conversation that helps to bind the *Life* together establishes the public Johnson, the "literary Colossus." The shadow behind it is the private Johnson, the figure of uneasy solitude, the business of whose life was to escape from his own thoughts—from the mind, as many agreed, that preyed on itself. Johnson had an unusual gift for spontaneous enjoyment—"What, is it you, you dogs! I'll have a frisk with you"—but recurrent melancholy, ranging from depression to despair, darkens his portrait throughout. Boswell has been criticized, perhaps rightly, for not sufficiently stressing Johnson's fear of madness; though as Mrs. Thrale admitted—and she had seen Johnson convulsed with anxiety—he could persuade no one to believe in his fear. But the *Life* is full of black expressions: "Je ne cherche rien, je n'espère rien"; "a kind of solitary wanderer in the wild of life . . . a gloomy gazer on a world to which I have little relation"; "I would consent to have a limb amputated to recover my spirits"; "terror and anxiety beset me." Most frightful of all was the approach of death. Yet just as Johnson fought to demonstrate superiority over his companions, so he struggled to keep mastery over himself. After citing one particularly troubled passage from Johnson's "private register," Boswell comments: "What philosophic heroism was it in him to appear with such manly fortitude to the world, while he was inwardly so distressed." Courage, Johnson once remarked, is considered the greatest of the natural virtues.

While it is the most banal of truisms that Boswell thought of Johnson as a father, in the *Life* he recurs to the formula he had used in the *Hebrides* and presents Johnson principally as "a majestic teacher of moral and religious wisdom." Johnson considered himself "as entrusted with a certain portion of truth" and he was willing to impart it. To begin with, he taught his fellow man "the boundless importance of the next life," with all the implications of that fundamental belief. Next, the most orthodox of eighteenth-century secular maxims: our first duty is to society, which is founded on respect for rank and property. Subordination (Johnson's favourite topic) is essential "to the fair and comfortable order of improved life."

When Johnson moves from these generalizations to specific issues of, say, politics, his views, so responsive to the times, now seem inert. It is clear that Johnson's reputation as a thinker cannot depend on particular opinions. One could fill an anthology with his "wrong" ideas on many subjects: Wilkes's expulsion from the House of Commons, the American Revolution, religious toleration, the prose of Swift and the poetry of Gray—on and on. But, as often noted, even when his views are outrageous Johnson makes them worth refuting.

It is Johnson the moralist, rather, whose stoic vision continues to command attention. His own achievements demonstrated some of the possibilities of life, while at the same time he continually insisted on its limitations. Life is "supported with impatience and quitted with reluctance"; it "is a progress from want to want, not from enjoyment to enjoyment"; even at best, "every man is to take existence on the terms on which it is given to him" and these terms may be highly restrictive. We are always hemmed in. As he warned Boswell, "Do not expect more from life than life will afford."

Conversation, as remarked earlier, often starting from a commonplace, elicits many of those observations "deep and sure in human nature," which show, as Boswell said, that Johnson's moral precepts were practical, appropriate to the recurring concerns of daily existence. His *dicta philosophi* (philosophical sayings) carry conviction because they are based on "a very attentive and minute survey of real life." They carry that weight of rightness, or at least of finality, which led Boswell to declare Johnson's "conversation was perhaps more admirable than even his writings, however excellent."

It is almost exhilarating when Johnson concludes, near the end of the *Life*, that existence is far more miserable than happy: this judgement offers the solidity of facing the worst. And in any case benevolence, which Johnson once defined as the chief duty of social beings, is a constant in this world, as is our hope of immortality in the next. Boswell lightens this austere outlook by stressing Johnson's fierce Anglican commitment—he is a militant and triumphant defender of the faith—and his constant practical exertions on behalf of deserving and undeserving alike. And Boswell repeatedly shows the gloomy moralist seizing with avidity the pleasures of the day.

Other heroes face the unusual; Johnson confronts the ordinary. His finest bit of advice came late in his intimacy with Boswell: whatever good breeding requires you to say, "My dear friend, clear your *mind* of cant." Johnson is a hero of awareness, of the examined life. And together with awareness, integrity; Johnson is never just the same, yet he is always of a piece, and always himself.

The most significant lesson Johnson offers is the example of his own life, and nowhere more so than in its close. A stroke was followed by the intermeshing pains of insomnia, asthma, and dropsy; he was deprived not only of the Thrales but of his familiar household companions, Levett and Mrs. Williams; others might consider him "the venerable sage" serenely abstracted from the world, but he faced the realities of sickness and solitude. His irritability was more apparent, his fear of death more immediate when, as he said, mortality presented its formidable frown, but he continued to cling tightly to life. Reynolds's last portrait of Johnson, "with its fallen lip and suffering indomitable eyes," catches the essence of this final struggle.

Death is the culmination of the old man's story as marriage is of the young man's, and Boswell leaves Johnson to recount his own last summer and autumn, through a series of letters that go over and over the same pathetic ground of declining health and lessening hope. But he remained intellectually alert and emotionally responsive: "Sir," he said to one friend, "I look upon every day to be lost in which I do not make a new acquaintance." To the last he maintained his "animated and lofty spirit." When hope ceased, he refused further medicines, even opiates, so that he could render up his soul to God unclouded.

Johnson finally is a hero as he emerges in his strengths and weaknesses—in the light and shade of Boswell's biography—because he grappled in extreme form with the beasts that can menace anyone: poverty, disease, loneliness, melancholy, sexual frustration, religious doubt, fear of insanity, dread of the inevitability of death. But his determination to survive and his willingness to assume responsibility for himself, to manage his mind and to keep control of his life, persisted to the end. This is a picture of Johnson that can be put to use.

IV

Boswell says, "I love to exhibit sketches of my illustrious friend by various eminent hands," and these reminiscences, especially of the not-so-eminent William Maxwell and Bennet Langton, are valuable additions to his account. But Johnson is more directly defined in the context of conversation: in sharp, varied interchanges with Garrick and Goldsmith, in reconciliation with Wilkes, in his many moods—angry, critical, loving—with Langton. He appears least clearly vis-à-vis Burke, whose fuzzy presentation is one of the Life's major disappointments.

Johnson's principal interlocutor, of course, is Boswell himself, and though in the Dedication he emphatically warns against identifying Boswell the author with Boswell the character, that confusion has always been the easiest way of misreading the Life. Certainly Boswell the author demonstrates a remarkable intelligence. As F. A. Pottle says: "The easy and delighted comprehension which [Boswell's] dramatic record shows at every point can be explained only by assuming that he had a mind that stretched parallel to Johnson's throughout the whole range of topics discussed."

Intelligence was matched to an equally remarkable ability to get what he perceived down on paper. "With how small a speck does a painter give life to an eye," Boswell had observed long before he came to write the *Life*, and this touch he imitated in the precision of his own detail. Yet he is careful not to let his phrasing call attention to itself. If, as Ruskin said, the symmetry of Johnson's style is "as of thunder answering from two horizons," then Boswell's style is as limitlessly transparent as the sky. The effect, often remarked, is to convince the reader that no medium intervenes between him and the scene being described, though Boswell has shaped it with care.

Here is the opening of one scene:

> Garrick played round [Johnson] with a fond vivacity, taking hold
> of the breasts of his coat and, looking up in his face with a lively
> archness, complimented him on the good health which he seemed
> then to enjoy; while the sage, shaking his head, beheld him with
> a gentle complacency.

The physical movement makes its own point, the playing round Johnson, taking hold of the breasts of his coat, as the small Garrick (he seems to have been no more than 5′4″) looks up at the 6′ Johnson. These details recalling their long intimacy—who else would have dared take Johnson by the lapels?—are shaded by phrases, "fond vivacity" and "lively archness," that suggest Garrick's mixture of attitudes: polite congratulation, fondness, play-acting—Garrick notoriously play-acted all the time—and the overtones of other responses: detachment, self-consciousness, even a touch of irony. In contrast Johnson, abstracted as "the sage," stands almost immobile—the fox plays round the hedgehog—but his reaction is ambiguous: is the shaking of the head a disclaimer of health or an intimation that he sees through Garrick's posing? "Gentle complacency" (French, *complaisance*, the manners of the well-bred) at least implies a benevolent if wary attitude. This tiny sketch, which occupies only a sentence, vibrates with the depth of a celebrated, complex friendship, while adding one more element to it.

To examine even so short a passage minutely is like concentrating on the brushwork of a Cézanne, or freezing a film to examine individual frames. But the ease and naturalness of Boswell's style carries us along quickly; we are not meant to stop to analyse the ebb and flow of suggestion underneath the clear verbal surface, to become explicitly aware of all the possibilities one sentence contains. The casual tone, the fluid movement, hide the subtle complications that give the scene its fullness, just as the elegant straightforwardness of Pope's couplets conceals some of the most difficult of English poetry.

The re-creation of even so brief an interchange requires a mind alert to the nuances of social behaviour, attuned to the intricate play of relationships. Yet if Boswell displays this kind of insight, what of the Boswell who could write himself down an ass? As in the *Hebrides*, Boswell's success has been, in part at least, his undoing: since Boswell the character is so clearly and fully developed it becomes difficult to keep in mind that Boswell the author observes him with some of the detachment with which he observes his other characters. And certain of Boswell's personal qualities, observable in the character portrayed, were very helpful to the author: vividness of sensation, openness of perception, immediacy and concreteness of response. Because he is unusually honest with himself, he can see others better for what they are. His plasticity, his ability to take on the tone of his company, even the childlikeness that can disregard received notions of decorum: all these contribute to the writing.

Boswell the questioner, manipulator, and stage manager, also has evident links to Boswell the author, but in revealing these roles to the audience, Boswell reinforces the persona of the "artless I," which he was willing to adopt once more because here, as in the *Hebrides*, it brought out Johnson so well. In remarking this persona for the final time, it should be stressed that this was an accepted technique, a possibility inherent in the "plain" or "simple" style that Hugh Blair, whose lectures on rhetoric Boswell had attended at the University of Edinburgh, called "naïveté":

> That sort of amiable ingenuity [ingenuousness] or undisguised openness, which seems to give us some degree of superiority over the person who shows it; a certain infantine simplicity which we love in our heart, but which displays some features of the character that we think we could have art enough to hide; and which, therefore, always leads us to smile at the person who discovers [reveals] this character.

Only once, at the end of the *Life*, does Boswell mention the "peculiar plan of his biographical undertaking," at the point where he offers his apologies "if he should be thought to have obtruded himself too much" on the reader's attention. But clearly from the beginning he had been aware of his special place in the story, and willing to take the risks of misapprehension that prominence entailed. Like Johnson's, his failings are more strongly marked than his virtues. He reveals that at times he was vain, snobbish, insecure, insatiably curious (a more admirable trait in a biographer than in a friend), and intrusive; he tells how he drank and misbehaved. The *Life* also provides full evidence that most people found him intelligent, attractive, good humoured, perceptive, and excellent company: as Johnson said, Boswell was welcome wherever he went.

What has really damaged Boswell's reputation is the direction in which he extends self-revelation. Like most of us Boswell sometimes acted very foolishly, but while other writers would bury such moments as deeply as possible, he is willing to exploit them if they can be turned to use—and, occasionally, it must be admitted, when they cannot. Boswell's eagerness to thrust his faults forward can become disturbing. He quotes Johnson as saying, "There is something noble in publishing truth, though it condemns one's self"; there can also be something exhibitionistic about it. While it is inaccurate to infer that Boswell had no sense of shame, he had less than most people.

Yet it is also easy to exaggerate the extent to which Boswell depreciates himself, as his detractors, who perhaps like him are insecure and self-conscious, are liable to do. Gray's remark that the title of the "Memoirs of Pascal Paoli" should have been "A Dialogue between a Green Goose and a Hero" evolved into the paradox that Macaulay made explicit: Boswell wrote a great book *because* he was a fool, a paradox that a moment's thought shows is a contradiction. Great books are written by great authors. That's how we recognize a great author: he has written a great book.

"I surely have the art of writing agreeably," Boswell told Temple, with very considerable understatement. Boswell had a much more remarkable gift, an almost mysterious power, what G. O. Trevelyan spoke of as

> that rare faculty (whose component elements the most distin-
> guished critics have confessed themselves unable to analyse),
> which makes every composition of Boswell's readable, from what
> he intended to be a grave argument on a point of law, down to
> his most slipshod verses and his silliest letters.

Boswell does show a rare faculty, both in general outlook and the ability to express it. Trevelyan's comment leads towards Proust's insight: style is not a question of technique but of vision. The interrelationship of vision and technique is ultimately impenetrable; it is impossible to say *where* or *how* Boswell came by his power to look at the world as he did, but, in his case, technique is so much an externalization of vision that one is tempted to agree with Croce that the two are identical.

What can be grasped is the world Boswell created in the *Life*, which opens out in time and scope as the title promises: "The whole exhibiting a view of literature and literary men in Great Britain, for near half a century during which [Johnson] flourished." Unlike the *Hebrides*, where movement and change of setting are indispensable, the scene here hardly varies: the dining-room, the drawing-room, and the tavern; seldom out-of-doors and rarely a glimpse of the bedchamber. Yet the *Life* never seems limited; it pours forth a variety of character and daily incident that no novel of the time can match.

If interest in certain contemporary topics (luxury, subordination, emigration, slavery) is now extinct, the *Life*'s figures have something still memorable to say about enduring ones: politics, religion, marriage, friendship, melancholy, death, and relations between the sexes. If the *Life* gives ample credit to misery, Boswell also fills it with enjoyment, as in the gathering at Mrs. Garrick's when he "whispered to Mrs. Boscawen, 'I believe this is as much as can be made of life' "; and at the level of social happiness it is. The *Life* is lively with the ordinary round of eating, talking, and visiting; it is a study in vitality: a crowded canvas of animated figures, against the background of London, representing the full tide of human existence.

The world of the *Life* is unified by Boswell's sensibility, and when seen as the transformation of life into art it becomes all the more impressive: from an existence marked by distress, long delays, half-willed actions, bad faith and broken promises, hastily snatched pleasures, wild illusions, the daily impediments of vanity, intemperance, lust, and despair, he has constructed with confident firmness a serene, generous world in which character and incident appear in undistorted perspective. The poet, as Sidney says, turns Nature's brazen world into a golden one. Yet rather than an invented world Boswell's is a fully realized one, which resists reduction to the much more selective constructs of fiction. And the *Life*, like the *Hebrides*, is very much literature of the world we know: Boswell took great pleasure in its daily operations and he left its rough edges. He was a connoisseur of the quotidian.

Carlyle, the most acute as well as the most absurd of Boswell's critics, attributed his greatness as a writer to his "open loving heart." The phrase is romantically indefinite but also highly suggestive, especially if expanded into terms we feel more at ease with. The delight Montaigne had taken in exploring his own mind, Boswell took in exploring the world of society. They had much in common, as Boswell insisted: urgent curiosity—about the familiar as well as the strange—combined with detachment, shrewdness, tolerance, and geniality. Very little human was alien to them. Boswell also could assimilate others, let them "sink in" on him, and represent them with a full sense of their humanity. When he presents his characters, he does not interpose his personality between us and them: they stand life-size. Most of the time he saves his moralizing for the footnotes.

A friend of mine remarks that if God wrote a novel it would be *Anna Karenina*. Certain writers—Chaucer, Shakespeare, George Eliot, Tolstoi—have the ability to suggest that they depict, in heightened consciousness, the world of normal vision, the world we share because it is created by the overlapping of our separate ways of perceiving existence. Boswell also projects normal vision, and though he does not compare with these wonderful writers in strength of invention or depth of imagination, he approaches them in power of realization. As W. K. Wimsatt says, he is "a visionary of the real."

Boswell's vision of his world is so convincing that it has overflowed to help colour an epoch. Just as we tend to see the Scottish world through Burns or Scott, and the Victorians through Dickens, so the atmosphere of the *Life* suffuses our sense of later eighteenth-century England. Boswell says himself that he Johnsonized the land, and it is because of him we identify this period as the Age of Johnson. At the same time Boswell is unique. In snatches later writers can reword him amusingly, as when Lamb says that "the author of *The Rambler* used to make inarticulate animal noises over a favourite food." But attempts to reproduce Boswell's tone and viewpoint in an extended work fail; even Thackeray, in *The Virginians* and *Henry Esmond*, produced only pastiche, in which the picturesque distances and the quaint diminishes the eighteenth-century world.

If you have a mean, pedantic spirit you will write a mean, pedantic biography, no matter who your subject is. And the reader will infer your character from your work. By the same reasoning, if a writer realizes a world notable for its sense of spaciousness, its fullness of presentation, its rightness of proportion, then these qualities dominate his deepest vision of life. Carlyle argued that Boswell's *Life of Johnson* was "the best possible resemblance of a Reality; like the very image thereof in a clear mirror." Several of Johnson's friends were talented writers; several sensed or knew that he was an heroic figure. But only Boswell, with his acute intelligence, his brilliant technique, and his open loving heart, could fully realize that greatness.

V

In his "Memoirs," published immediately after the *Life of Johnson*, Boswell stated with understandable complacency that the *Life* had been "received by the world with extraordinary approbation." It was a best seller: of the 1,750 copies printed, 888 had been sold in the first month after publication. And it was soon trailing a string of parodies, a good omen of success.

Not everyone liked it, of course. The Critical Reviewer complained of dull anecdotes and the impropriety of reporting private conversations. Both subject and biographer displeased him: Johnson for "brutal severity," and Boswell for "affected self-importance" and "passive fawning insensibility." Some of Johnson's friends objected once more to the revelation of his weaknesses and eccentricities. The eighteenth century liked to stick its heroes, whatever their private failings, into marble togas, literally in the case of Bacon's sculpture of Johnson in St. Paul's. But, from the start, Boswell had been determined to write a life not a panegyric: when Hannah More— to repeat a well-known story—"begged he would mitigate some of [Johnson's] asperities," Boswell told her "roughly" that "he would not cut off his claws, not make a tiger a cat to please anybody." As Dr. Burney later remarked in his usual mild way, Boswell had numerous good qualities but delicacy was not among them: "He was equally careless what was said of himself or what he said of others."

Percy would have sworn to the last statement. Not only did he stand displayed as a thin-skinned sycophant in the wonderfully funny and humiliating account of the Pennantian controversy, but he seemed a special target elsewhere. In particular, when Boswell told Johnson that Percy was writing a history of the wolf in Great Britain, Johnson asked why he didn't write a history of the grey or Hanover rat, so called because it had made its appearance in the country at the same time as the House of Hanover. JOHNSON. "'I should like to see *The History of the Grey Rat* by Thomas Percy, D.D., Chaplain in Ordinary to His Majesty' (laughing immoderately)." Nor was Percy pacified by Boswell's comment: "Thus could he indulge a luxuriant sportive imagination when talking of a friend whom he loved and esteemed." After the publication of the *Life*, Percy could hardly be persuaded to speak to Boswell or to attend meetings of The Club when Boswell was to be present.

And one can hardly blame others for taking offence. Richard Hurd, Bishop of Worcester, for example, spoke fiercely to his commonplace book about "a striking likeness of a confident, overweening, dictatorial pedant, though of parts and learning; and of a weak, shallow, submissive admirer of such a character, deriving a vanity from that very admiration." But then Hurd had learned from Boswell's work that he had been Warburton's toady, and when "well-advanced in life" had engaged in "unjust and acrimonious abuse of two men of eminent merit."

Even Wilkes, who might have been expected to relish the *Life*'s high spirits, had mixed feelings about it. He told Boswell it was "a wonderful book," but wrote more openly to his daughter (during a dry spell): "The earth is as thirsty as Boswell, and as cracked in many places as he certainly is in one. His book, however, is that of an entertaining madman." Wilkes may not have cared for the remark that his reconciliation with Johnson reminded the Bishop of Killaloe of the lion lying down with the goat. But, to do him justice, he had objected to the *Hebrides* also. Perhaps his literary tastes, unlike some of his writings, had always been conventional.

There were others who damned Johnson himself, literary tyrant and Hottentot, "puffy pensioner" with his "insolent bigotry," along with Boswell. Horace Walpole spoke for some when he wrote:

> With a lumber of learning and some strong parts, Johnson was an odious and mean character. . . . His manners were sordid, supercilious, and brutal; his style ridiculously bombastic and vicious; and, in one word, with all the pedantry he had all the gigantic littleness of a country schoolmaster.

And others grew angry on behalf of their friends. Norton Nicholls, who had been one of Gray's intimates, wrote to Temple (21 July 1791): "I have run through Boswell's *Life of Johnson* and can never forgive the disrespect shown to Mr. Gray. . . . Indeed, I never before met with (to use a gentle term) so unguarded a publication."

Boswell's own friends joined in the criticism of one aspect of the *Life*, its depiction of Goldsmith as a highly talented writer who often made a fool of himself. But Boswell did not make a comic butt of Goldsmith; Goldsmith had made one of himself. As Reynolds, his best friend, admitted, Goldsmith would "sing, stand upon his head [or] dance about the room" to attract attention. Nor did anyone question that Goldsmith spoke and acted precisely as Boswell said he did; one can object at most that Boswell is just to him rather than generous. On the other hand, Boswell could have been faulted more than he was for his tiresome sniping at Hawkins and Mrs. Piozzi, and for using the few opportunities available to make personal attacks on Gibbon, whose contempt for religion pressed on an exposed nerve.

But the common reader found the *Life* irresistible, and so did a majority of the reviewers. Reporting that it had been "received by the public with extraordinary avidity," John Nichols, in the *Gentleman's Magazine,* struck the general note: "a literary portrait is here delineated which all who knew the original will allow to be THE MAN HIMSELF." Ralph Griffiths, in the *Monthly*

Review, was "astonished at Mr. B.'s industry and perseverance!—to say nothing of the multiplicity and variety of his own occasional [directed to specific occasions] and pertinent observations." Johnson appeared "in his mind's undress. . . . All is natural, spontaneous, and unreserved." Griffiths urged that any reader would say to "the reporter": "Give us *all*, suppress nothing; lest in rejecting that which in your estimation may seem to be of inferior value, you unwarily throw away gold with the dross."

The *Life* was so entertaining, so delightful, so quick to capture and hold attention that no one realized immediately that it was a major addition to English literature. The *English Review* considered it a great gift to the lovers of light amusement: "The airy garrulity of the narrative will effectually recommend these volumes to volatile and desultory readers." The serious presumably turned to such works published that year as Beloe's translation of Herodotus and Cowper's of Homer, both given longer reviews in the *Gentleman's Magazine* than the *Life*. Like the *Hebrides*, the *Life* was not received at its true value because it lacked literary dignity.

But as early as 1795, the year of Boswell's death, Robert Anderson, with strong assistance from a letter by Malone in the *Gentleman's Magazine*, had arrived at a reasonably accurate estimate:

> With some venial exceptions on the score of egotism and indiscriminate admiration, his work exhibits the most copious, interesting, and finished picture of the life and opinions of an eminent man that was ever executed, and is justly esteemed one of the most instructive and entertaining books in the English language.
>
> The eccentricities of Mr. Boswell, it is useless to detail. They have already been the subject of ridicule in various different forms and publications by men of superficial understanding and ludicrous fancy. [What follows is Malone.] Many have supposed him to be a mere relater of the sayings of others; but he possessed considerable intellectual powers for which he has not had sufficient credit. It is manifest to every reader of any discernment that he could never have collected such a mass of information and just observations on human life as his very valuable work contains, without great strength of mind and much various knowledge; as he never could have displayed his collections in so lively a manner had he not possessed a very picturesque imagination or, in other words, had he not had a very happy turn for poetry, as well as for humour and wit.

Just a few years later James Northcote recognized that "very few books in the English language bid fairer for immortality than [Boswell's] *Life of Johnson*." Macaulay's pronouncement in 1831, issued with his usual flat self-sufficiency, fixed its reputation: "Eclipse is first, and the rest nowhere." At the time of publication Boswell himself must have cherished the Latin verses contributed by Sandy from Eton, and Jamie from Westminster [his sons], welcoming the long-awaited emergence of the *Life*. Jamie's verses have not survived, but Sandy's begin bravely if unsyntactically:

> Adveniit tempus jamjam, quae musa tacebit,
>   Quae non cantabit gloria magna modis?
>
> [Now the time approaches, what muse will be silent,
> What muse will not sing your great glory in its measures?]

But no sign of public approval could match George III's remark: "Mr. Burke told me it was the most entertaining book he had ever read."

Contemporary objections to the *Life* have, or should have, faded with the years. But modern critics have found new charges to make. One, that Boswell suppressed some materials and bowdlerized others, is of course the exact opposite of contemporary complaint, and shows profound ignorance of eighteenth-century standards of decorum. In general, the question, "How much should a biographer tell?" is a non-issue: any biographer like Boswell who wants to present his subject whole tells all he can find out, thinks pertinent, and hopes he can get away with. A second charge, that Boswell was inaccurate, is almost ludicrous when his performance is compared with those of his rivals. For his time Boswell made an extraordinary effort to collect the facts, and the more facts the more chance for error. No biographer gets every fact right, nor do any of Boswell's few, easily corrected errors substantively affect his portrait of Johnson. A third charge, that Boswell slighted Mrs. Thrale's significance, has more merit. But circumstances—closeness to the events related, their rivalry, and the general conviction of Johnson's friends that she had deserted him in the shabbiest manner—made a just appraisal out of the question. Boswell assumes rather than brings out properly her central role in the last twenty years of Johnson's life.

A serious problem for some modern Johnsonians is that Johnson the conversationalist obscures Johnson the writer. It may be true that Burke declared Boswell's *Life* would be a greater monument to Johnson than all his writings; it is certain that both Macaulay and Carlyle, in the nineteenth-century vein of thinking the poet more significant than the poem, emphatically agreed. But even though Boswell himself found Johnson's conversation more impressive than his writings, he also praised Johnson's works highly—he said in his journal that they were the food of his soul—and surely he is not responsible if others have either agreed or disagreed with him.

In contrast to the old misconception that Boswell was no more than a reporter, an occasional modern will say that while Boswell's material is worthwhile, he had the temerity to provide a commentary; he interprets what he records. Here is a well-known example from 1784: "[Johnson] bore the journey very well, and seemed to feel himself elevated as he approached Oxford, that magnificent and venerable seat of learning, orthodoxy, and Toryism." Isn't this sheer Boswell? How dare he pretend to know what was going on in Johnson's mind? But Boswell's statement is modest; he says merely that Johnson "seemed to feel himself elevated." Thousands of biographers have looked far more confidently into their subjects' heads without incurring reproach. And Boswell was there as his censurers were not; he could see Johnson's expression and sense his mood. Boswell had a right, perhaps a duty, to interpret Johnson's reaction.

It may seem curious that Boswell, almost two hundred years after his death, is sometimes attacked as if the critic held a personal grudge. But Johnson still exerts such a powerful attraction that sibling rivalry continues to burn, with Boswell as the envied and hated eldest brother. In more than one instance, Boswell has been vigorously abused at the very same time that his material was being copiously appropriated.

The adequacy of any depiction of Johnson will always remain a matter of individual judgement. Yet assessment of Boswell's portrayal involves more than subjective reactions. It has to take into account such factors as contemporary testimony to the power and fidelity of his image of Johnson, the testimony not merely of reviewers but of men who knew Johnson very well, like Adams, Malone, or Reynolds, who said that "every word in it might be depended upon as if given upon oath." In addition, though Boswell shapes his particulars he never invents them, while his closest rivals among English biographers, Lockhart and Strachey, were notoriously indifferent to mere fact. As soon as credibility is damaged, to some indefinable extent our trust is reduced and so our pleasure in the work.

Finally, it has been objected that Boswell spent no more than 425 days with Johnson, so he could not have known him as well as Hawkins or Mrs. Thrale. Certainly Hawkins knew him much longer, and Mrs. Thrale more intimately, but like most of us they were too engrossed in their own dear selves to give the equally clear-sighted and obsessive attention to another that Boswell paid to Johnson. The *Life* in itself sufficiently refutes such criticism, but this line of argument can be profitably pursued. Boswell recorded Johnson directly and extensively over a period of 21 years. For much of that time he knew he was going to write Johnson's biography. For over three months during their Hebridean tour, they lived together in very close quarters. And though Boswell failed to make notes about many of the days they spent with each other, those days helped to impart a rich familiarity to the ones he does record. Imagine how valuable it would be to a modern biographer to spend even one day with Johnson! Imagine having watched him, listened to him, been grumbled at and blessed and hugged to him like a sack!

Gossip

Patricia Meyer Spacks

Telling stories about human lives, biography, like published letters, encourages the temptation to interpret, the lure of "finding out," the fantasy of knowing. Unlike letters, it offers coherent narrative, product of a structuring intelligence other than the reader's. Delineating someone who has actually lived in the world, this narrative claims the status of "truth." Biography has been considered a branch of history, a source of information about politics and about the underpinnings of public events. It has traditionally provided models of conduct, depictions of embodied excellence which readers may aspire to approach in their own lives. More recently, the "debunking" biography has assured us of inadequacies concealed behind public façades. Ernst Kris's demonstration that ancient biographies of artists consistently purveyed the same stories about different subjects suggests that biographies may partake also of fiction ("biography originates in myth," Kris says); yet although the patterns of "factual" narrative derive from legend, from cultural assumption, from individual wish and will, beneath those patterns, readers persistently believe, lies a substratum of facticity. Reading a novel, experienced readers expect to understand the world better for encountering imaginative transformations of it; they do not anticipate learning about actual people in society. Belief that biography affords opportunity for such learning partly explains its ambiguous literary status:

if the genre exists primarily to convey information, perhaps it does not merit aesthetic assessment.

One can ignore claims of facticity and treat biography as a literary genre like any other, a verbal structure subject to verbal analysis. (William Dowling's recent exegeses of Boswell, for example, adopt this procedure.) Yet to deny altogether what has long constituted biography's ground of justification seems, if up-to-date, also perverse. An adequate aesthetic, like an adequate epistemology, of biography would take into account the text's claim to relay historical fact, to constitute history of an individual—and would go beyond that claim, to define the art of such history.

The pleasure of reading biography, like that of reading letters, derives from the universal hunger to penetrate other lives. Plausibility, consequently, constitutes biography's fundamental requirement: not necessarily literal accuracy, but the kind of interpretation that "makes sense," a story about human life fitting our convictions about the shapes life assumes. To assess the plausibility of a biographical text thus may involve hidden aesthetic judgment. Decisions about a narrative's likely degree of accuracy often conceal feelings and ideas about appropriateness, beliefs about the form of experience derived as much from fiction as from life.

The narrator in biography functions as source and guardian of knowledge, in ways comparable to novelistic narrators. The novelist, however, invents characters; the biographer only interprets them. The biographical storyteller must convince the reader—particularly the reader aware of more than a single biography of a given subject—of the narrator's right and power to control the story. Such authority and power depend not only on the forms into which narrators fit their narratives but on the distance they maintain: between biographer and subject, between biographer and reader, consequently between subject and reader.

This matter of distance proves complicated in biography. The biographer cannot risk too much coziness. As Frank Brady observes, "If [biography] takes the form of a fictional reconstruction of the thoughts and actions of real persons, it is usually dismissed as a hybrid hardly worth despising." The narrator must not claim to know more than s/he can know; biographical narrators cannot conspicuously indulge imagination, cannot convey the immediate internal specificity of character which their novelistic counterparts provide. The reader's trust will depend largely on the narrator's precise control of plausible distance. The narrator stabilizes both storyteller's and reader's relation to the biographical subject. Authority does not necessarily derive from the preservation of great height: the biographer in a superior position, declaring possession of knowledge that enables interpretation; the narrator may claim, rather, the special awareness of intimacy. Readers' interest in biography as a genre may reflect yearning to grasp how other human beings resemble us or the wish to examine closely an individual specimen of human life, without conscious reference to the self. (Interest in a specific biography, of course, often depends on pre-existent concern with its subject.) We may wish to reflect upon the greatness of the renowned, or to encounter their insufficiencies. The biographer's choices of tone and stance and of detail will determine the relationship established by the text, the boundaries separating subject from reader, the nature as well as the substance of interpretation.

Late in his life, Dr. Johnson verbalized a distinction between physical and moral truth. "Physical truth, is, when you tell a thing as it actually is. Moral truth, is, when you tell a thing sincerely and precisely as it appears to you. I say such a one walked across the street; if he really did so, I told a physical truth. If I thought so, though I should have been mistaken, I told a moral truth." Biographers deal in both kinds of truth; and, as the terms of Johnson's definition imply, they can hardly distinguish between them since in both cases belief informs their telling. Nor, often, can the reader distinguish.

The biographical equivalent of "moral truth" involves issues more important than crossing the street. Interpretation of character and event derives from how things *appear* to the biographer. To call this truth of appearance, as it manifests itself in biography, *moral* directs attention not only to the conviction underlying it, but to the fact that the sub-stratum of interpretation, however concealed, often involves moral judgment. (I am, of course, extending the implications of Johnson's distinction between "moral" and "physical" truth.) The biographer's belief in the subject's human value or meretriciousness informs the life story and shapes interpretations. Dr. Johnson takes a trip to Oxford, Birmingham, Lichfield, and Ashbourne in the fall of 1781. Boswell points out, with a slap at Sir John Hawkins (another of Johnson's early biographers), that "very good reasons might be given [for this trip] in the conjectural yet positive manner of writers, who are proud to account for every event which they relate." He confines himself to quoting Johnson's own comments: the traveler says he hardly knows the motives of his journey, he refers to his love for his schoolmate Edmund Hector, and he claims a desire to show a good example in his native town of Lichfield "by frequent attendance on publick worship." Walter Jackson Bate, reporting the same excursion, also quotes Johnson on his doubts about motivation and on his love for Hector. But Bate adds, "The people he wished to see at Lichfield . . . were getting old. . . . It was here, among these people, that his roots had been. He was instinctively turning to them now that he felt himself losing what had been so important in his later life." Bate does not cite Johnson's sentence about wishing to provide a good example.

Boswell's ostentatious refusal to interpret implies his judgment (by no means consistent throughout the *Life*) that Johnson's veracity and integrity make him the ultimate authority on his own actions. Bate's interpretation emerges in declarative sentences, not formally distinct from sentences narrating known events. Such a statement as "He was instinctively turning to them now . . ." exemplifies one kind of "moral truth" in biography: a sincere and precise telling of what to the biographer appears to be the case. It too implies moral evaluation: for Johnson, human ties had powerful meaning. Boswell's inclusion, Bate's omission of the remark about public worship point up their different grounds of judgment. For Bate, as for most twentieth-century readers, no doubt, Johnson's desire to worship in public in order to improve his townspeople sounds like rationalization. For Boswell, the profession of piety heightens Johnson's moral authority.

To come to adequate terms with an individual biography involves assessing—or at least locating—its art, its morality, and its knowledge. All three customarily resemble but rarely duplicate their novelistic equivalents. The *art* of biography, as of the novel, inheres in narrative—the creation of a persuasive story and of characters who make it plausible—but in biography facts restrict narrative form. The *moral assumptions* of a given biography may of course duplicate those of any other genre, though the concern with people who have actually lived and with literal details of their lives often encourages more ethical strictness than do the looser imaginings of fiction. The *knowledge* of biography includes not only the imaginative, interpretive knowledge fiction provides but facts of individual history. In every aspect, then, biography's claimed connection with actuality modifies its manifestations.

Two pairs of biographies will help to elucidate these claims: an eighteenth- and a twentieth-century life of Samuel Johnson, [and, not included here,] a nineteenth- and a twentieth-century account of Charlotte Brontë. In both pairings, the author of the earlier work, a friend of the subject, claims friendship's special knowledge and functions as apologist. The two twentieth-century biographies share psychological orientations and a technique of analyzing texts as testimony of inner experience. To look at these works under the aspect of gossip will not construct an aesthetic, an epistemology, or a morality of biography; it will not even produce a comprehensive reading of texts. But gossip provides a way of focusing on all three aspects of biography and of demonstrating relationships among them.

No less an authority than Horace Walpole links Boswell's *Johnson* with gossip. "Boswell's book is gossipping," he writes Mary Berry, "but having numbers of proper names, would be more readable, at least by me, were it reduced from two volumes to one." A cryptic footnote, by the modern editors, to this cryptic comment claims that Walpole meant it as a compliment. Walpole's remark seems to imply that, delightful though he finds gossip, too many proper names interfere with readability: less would be more.

I suggested [elsewhere] that gossip resembles an action of knowing, taking *action* in its Aristotelian sense: a unifying explanatory structure for a sequence of events. Gossiping speakers exchange and interpret information in order—for good reasons or bad—to enlarge their grasp of someone else's experience and thus, ideally, better to understand their own. In a more immediate sense, gossip constitutes an action of telling. Without telling, it would not exist.

James Boswell, like all biographers, claims to know a great deal about another person and to tell what he knows. His modes of knowing and of telling connect *The Life of Samuel Johnson, LL.D.*, for all its dignity, with gossip.

Boswell distinguishes himself from other writers about Johnson (Hester Thrale Piozzi and Sir John Hawkins) and associates himself with his mentor by claiming absolute veracity. He works endlessly, he says, to verify allegations; he seeks material everywhere. Implicitly he differentiates his work from Hawkins' by suggesting his own superiority to gossip: "Sir John Hawkins's ponderous labours, I must acknowledge, exhibit a *farrago*, of which a considerable portion is not devoid of entertainment to the lovers of literary gossiping. . . ." On the other hand, Boswell incorporates into his own text versions of Johnson supplied by such others as Bennet Langton and Joshua Reynolds; he records in detail stories he will subsequently deny, thus satisfying his (and the presumed reader's) pleasure in a good anecdote without damaging his claim of accuracy; and, as he frequently acknowledges, he reports the tiniest details about his friend.

"Much pleasant conversation passed," Boswell writes (of a meeting of The Club on 30 April 1773), "which Johnson relished with great good humour. But his conversation alone, or what led to it, or was interwoven with it, is the business of this work." Johnson suggests the moral function of his own talk when he justifies himself for refusing to respond to demands for more writing by claiming the same efficacity for his conversation and his writing: only the size of the audience differs. "Now, Sir, the good I can do by my conversation bears the same proportion to the good I can do by my writings, that the practice of a physician, retired to a small town, does to his practice in a great city." Boswell, as he promises, makes it his business to record what Johnson says. Rarely does the reported conversation resemble gossip. Indeed, the operative definition of *conversation* implies stress on ideas. When Boswell asks Johnson if good conversation occurred on a given occasion, the doctor replies, "No, Sir; we had *talk* enough, but no *conversation*; there was nothing *discussed*" (Boswell's italics). By *discussing* issues moral, philosophic, political, social, and literary, Johnson reveals the dimensions of his mind and justifies Boswell's hero-worship. Conversation, in Johnson's view (apparently in Boswell's as well), is combat. It involves competitive self-display, in which one person necessarily emerges triumphant. Johnson talks for victory, as he acknowledges; he will assume a position he does not hold so as to demonstrate his capacity to defend it. The object of conversation is to win. Johnson usually wins.

The value system implicit in this model of conversation utterly opposes the one I have declared characteristic of gossip. To interpret other participants as audience or metaphoric patients, passive recipients of the great man's wisdom, as Johnson does in claiming the "good" he can do by his conversation, or to see talkers as combatants neglects the possibility of fruitful mutual exchange, more likely to occur in what Johnson calls "talk" than in what he calls "conversation." As even Boswell stresses (less emphatically than Bate), Johnson demonstrated vast capacity for loyalty and concern, valuing his affectional ties. But for him conversation belonged more to the realm of war than of human love; gossip, despite its possible animosity toward the absent, asserts the participants' closeness.

Given this fact, and the equally obvious truth that Boswell's *Life* centers on combative conversation, it may seem odd to associate it with gossip. True, the biography contains many names and many stories about the people those names designate; it tells even more stories about unnamed "gentlemen" or "clergymen." (Only Johnson, however, becomes the object of what Clifford Geertz calls "thick description.") True, as I pointed out above, it reports hearsay evidence and dwells on minutiae of conduct and appearance, with the sanction of Johnson himself, who believed as firmly as Boswell in the illuminating power of detail. But more important than any of these facts is the dominant myth of heroism informing this biography: and the implications of heroism, like those of Johnsonian "conversation," do not readily associate themselves with gossip.

Boswell rarely misses an opportunity to declare his subject's virtually superhuman stature. Even before he meets Johnson, he confesses, he feels for him "a kind of mysterious veneration," which only increases upon close acquaintance. "During all the course of my long intimacy with him, my respectful attention never abated, and my wish to hear him was such, that I constantly watched every dawning of communication from that great and illuminated mind." The very house Johnson inhabits appears to Boswell's imagination "to be sacred to wisdom and piety." "I cannot help worshipping him," Boswell says to the historian William Robertson, who has expressed anxiety lest excessive admiration "spoil" Johnson, "he is so much superior to other men." The assumption of categorical superiority controls the entire work, which concludes with the vision of all the world revering Johnson as Boswell does: "Such was SAMUEL JOHNSON, a man whose talents, acquirements, and virtues, were so extraordinary, that the more his character is considered, the more he will be regarded by the present age, and by posterity, with admiration and reverence."

Yet *The Life of Samuel Johnson, LL.D.* would inhabit the imagination less powerfully if it comprised simple hagiography. Two obvious aspects of the book, to both of which the text itself calls attention, emphasize its actual tensions of purpose and attitude: the constant intrusion of Boswell as a character, and the frequent exposures of Johnson as at least briefly unkind, petty, fearful, or self-absorbed. One can incorporate both Boswell's insistent presence and Johnson's feet of clay into the dominant pattern of stress on the heroic: Boswell deliberately makes himself a foil to his subject's grandeur, playing the fool, we might say; and Johnson's comparatively minor weaknesses only underline his achieved strengths. Such explanations, however, though true as far as they go, fail to do justice to the biography's effect. Despite its claims that Johnson provides an appropriate object of veneration, the book reveals him as a struggling human being; and it insists on the drama implicit in telling the story of such a man. Its narrative, in other words, involves Boswell the writer and Johnson the fallible man. Boswell makes both himself and his hero into subjects of gossip: intimate anecdote, intimate speculation. And he demonstrates that gossip need not preclude glorification.

Vivid consciousness of biography's moral problematics informs the *Life*, with its implicit generic questions: why write, why read, biography? Although Johnson himself, in his *Rambler* essay on the subject, had offered moral justification (biography, by conveying intimate knowledge of other lives, helps us to know ourselves), he did not resolve all ambiguities. Boswell several times worries in print about whether a biographer should expose his subject's frailties. Johnson's precedent—he reported Parnell's and Addison's alcoholic excesses—justifies his biographer, but does not alleviate anxiety. After alleging Johnson's youthful sexual indulgence, the narrator remarks, "I am conscious that this is the most difficult and dangerous part of my biographical work, and I cannot but be very anxious concerning it. I trust that I have got through it, preserving at once my regard to truth,—to my friend,—and to the interests of virtue and religion." This threefold obligation suggests high-minded justification for biography. But problems remain. Boswell's anxiety, one may speculate, rises partly from self-suspicion. Maybe, despite his protestations, he wishes to reduce the stature of an uncomfortably gigantic figure. Perhaps people read biography not to confirm but to challenge the moral grandeur of larger-than-lifesize public figures. If a life story uncovers weakness and folly, does it not serve leveling impulses, the desire to emphasize the limits of human possibility so as to avoid the necessity of aspiration? The writer and the reader of biography may gratify malice and envy in the guise of serving truth, virtue, and religion. Where are truth's proper limits? Should everything known be told; should one seek knowledge no matter where the search leads? Need biography respect no privacies?

The issues implicit in such questions, the ambiguity of all possible answers, may remind us of similar issues, similar ambiguities, in discussions of gossip through the ages. Gossip too may seek and circulate truth—or, like biography on occasion, fiction in the guise of truth. Gossip, too, often purports to serve morality, to reinforce communal standards. It declares human interest in human beings, but it violates privacy and punctures pretensions. Enlarging knowledge and understanding, it yet may arouse uncomfortable doubts in its practitioners about the motivation and the propriety of their behavior. Moral ambiguity dogs it.

Boswell invites his reader into a relationship with similarities to the tie expressed and generated by gossip.

> Some time after this, upon his making a remark which escaped my attention, Mrs. Williams and Mrs. Hall were both together striving to answer him. He grew angry, and called out loudly, "Nay, when you both speak at once, it is intolerable." But checking himself, and softening, he said, "This one may say, though you *are* ladies." Then he brightened into gay humour, and addressed them in the words of one of the songs in "The Beggar's Opera."

"But two at a time there's no mortal can bear."
"What, Sir, (said I,) are you going to turn Captain Macheath?"
There was something as pleasantly ludicrous in this scene as can
be imagined. The contrast between Macheath, Polly, and Lucy—
and Dr. Samuel Johnson, blind, peevish Mrs. Williams, and lean,
lank, preaching Mrs. Hall, was exquisite.

This randomly chosen episode epitomizes Boswell's typical mode in relating
a verbal interchange of no obvious intrinsic significance. Dr. Johnson is
seventy-two years old at the time, Mrs. Hall (John Wesley's widowed sister)
and Anna Williams (a longtime pensioner of Johnson's) two or three years
older. As the *London Journal* reveals, Macheath, the dashing highwayman of
The Beggar's Opera, had been a favorite fantasy-model of Boswell in his youth.
Now, grown-up, Boswell perceives and gently exposes the discrepancy
between imagining and reality. There is no time in the unconscious, Freud
has told us; Dr. Johnson can fall into Macheath's role without feeling its
incongruity. Boswell evokes not only the ludicrous contrast between the
literal and the imagined cast of characters, but the subtler comedy of
Johnson's movement (anger—softening—brightening) from impatient anger
to self-reminder of the rules of gallantry to discovery of a literary allusion
that makes rebuke of ladies morally tolerable to him.

The art here involves more than that dramatic rendering often noted
as one of Boswell's literary gifts. Intimately connected with the biographer's
capacity for moral perception, it derives also from his ability to perceive
significance in the trivial. Not only his precise observation of what Johnson
does and says but his sensitivity to the psychic movement underlying shifts
in speech and action, his own emotional responsiveness, his ability to specify
sources of comedy—all contribute to the scene's rhetorical and dramatic
effect. Boswell tells a story, even (or especially) a tiny story, well and
interprets it well. If these embody the biographer's skills, they also epitomize
the gossip's. Boswell's narrations heighten the reader's hunger for every detail
about Johnson. The biographer provides a banquet of idiosyncrasy and urges
us to savor it. Johnson rarely gossips; but Boswell's reports of his discourse,
however dignified, become the substance of gossip by being incorporated
into the pattern of intense concentration on, and implicit or explicit
interpretation of, verbal and visual minutiae.

What I have said about Boswell applies, in varying degree, to biography
in general. Not all biographers possess Boswell's descriptive or dramatic
expertise or his memory, his obsessiveness, his analytic dexterity. But many
biographies, like Boswell's, invite their readers to dwell on and to seek

significance in human detail. The pleasure of biography can involve not only delight in finding out, but delight in the *process* of finding out, a process bearing striking resemblances to that of gossip.

Because the narrator bears primary responsibility for any intrusion, reading biography feels less like violating privacies than does reading letters. But biography too has liminal status, on the border between "literature" and "history," uncertainly justified by the quality of its narration or the degree of its accuracy. Boswell's version of biography involves another borderland as well, which many, but not all, biographies evoke: that between public and private. The two special aspects of the *Life* I noted previously, the narrator's constant intrusion into the narration and the combination of recurrent debunking with insistent idealization, both illuminate the special relation of public and private in this text. They also have their bearing on gossip.

Invoking "the present age" and "posterity" as sanctions for his own obsession, Boswell indicates—as he does repeatedly throughout the biography—his conviction that Johnson's status as public figure justifies detailed attention to his character and personality. As author of the *Dictionary*, which accomplished for England what academies of learned men had done for Italy and France, as the moral philosopher of *The Rambler*, as writer, finally, of the *Lives of the Poets*, which solidified new standards for biography and articulated a partial canon of English poetry, Johnson indeed belonged to the ages. The religious language of "worship" and "reverence" implicitly claims Johnson's superhuman stature. From one point of view, the biography exists to substantiate this stature and to gratify readers' yearnings for objects of idealization. Like Greek tragedy, this kind of biography shows someone elevated above mankind in general and demonstrates how his character becomes his fate.

The desire to worship and the desire for intimate knowledge oppose one another. As Boswell reveals Johnson scraping bits of orange peel, caressing his cat, losing his temper, fearing death and loneliness, appearing in public with shabby clothes and undersized wig, upholding untenable positions, abusing innocent bystanders and insulting Boswell himself—the reader, encountering emphatic evidence of human frailty, can no longer understand Johnson as saint or monument. As private man, the hero resembles other men. Intimate specificity modifies the myth of heroism. Gossip emphasizes what people hold in common, dwells on frailties, seeks the hidden rather than the manifest; heroism thrives on specialness and on public manifestation. Boswell proclaims his intimate relation with his subject. For the reader's attention to hundreds of pages of data and interpretation, he promises the reward of knowledge that will undermine public pretension. The intimacy he establishes with the reader parallels that he has won with Johnson. With Johnson, he feels himself the inferior: thirty-one years younger than his mentor, infinitely less accomplished. In imagined association with his reader, he assumes the superior position, source of information and interpretation. He also demonstrates the special sense in which he can claim superiority even to Johnson.

Boswell depicts himself in the text mainly as naïf, always deferring to Johnson's superior wisdom and experience. But increasingly also he presents himself as author, specifically as intending biographer, asking Johnson questions about his past, copying extracts from his diary, criticizing the inadequacy of friends who fail to write down what they hear. On page 380—fifty pages before the end—of the final volume of the *Life*, he remarks, "I now relieve the readers of this Work from any farther personal notice of its authour, who if he should be thought to have obtruded himself too much upon their attention, requests them to consider the peculiar plan of his biographical undertaking." He has just reported his own indisposition during the final months of Johnson's life and his consequent inability to correspond, has transcribed Johnson's final letter to him and complained about Johnson's rebukes to him for the melancholy the older man shared, and has assured his readers that Johnson "spoke of me on his death-bed, with affection, and I look forward with humble hope of renewing our friendship in a better world."

Boswell, of course, continues to "obtrude." The first-person-singular pronoun occurs regularly, even in critical observations; the biographer reminds us at every turn that all judgments and perceptions issue from his mind. He professes once more his "sacred love of truth" and declares his anxiety, in a sequence I have already quoted, about "the most difficult and dangerous part" of his work. He reports having read, without Johnson's knowledge, in his diary and sets down the subsequent dialogue ("apologizing for the liberty I had taken, [I] asked him if I could help it"). He bestows approval on William Windham, the statesman, for visiting the dying sage. He declares his own inability to express his feelings adequately: "I trust, I shall not be accused of affectation, when I declare, that I find myself unable to express all that I felt upon the loss of such a 'Guide, Philosopher, and Friend.'" Once more, he emphasizes the difficulty of his biographical task, after pointing out that the reader, by this time, "may be considered as well acquainted" with Johnson. In short, Boswell remains as much on hand as ever after he announces his disappearance.

The "peculiar plan" which Boswell invokes concentrates on developing the reader's intimacy with the subject. "Indeed I cannot conceive a more perfect mode of writing any man's life, than not only relating all the most important events of it in their order, but interweaving what he privately wrote, and said, and thought; by which mankind are enabled as it were to see him live, and to 'live o'er each scene' with him, as he actually advanced through the several stages of his life." He thus announces his intent of focusing both on the public and on the private. He does not, however, explain why double focus involves insistent self-presentation. Perhaps he would claim that he brings the reader into relation with the subject partly by representing his own relation. But my citations from the final fifty pages, all of which directly or indirectly concern Boswell's role as biographer, suggest another reason for the biography's partial concentration on its author. "To write the Life of him who excelled all mankind in writing the lives of others, and who, whether we consider his extraordinary endowments, or his various works, has been equalled by few in any age, is an arduous, and may be reckoned in me a presumptuous task." So the *Life* begins. However arduous, however presumptuous the task, Boswell performs it. However unequaled Johnson's attainments, Boswell takes possession of them in prose. He assumes the power of representation, he tells the story, he assigns the meanings.

The stability thus achieved opposes gossip's essential insecurity. But inasmuch as Boswell makes his search for such stability a subject of his narrative, dramatizing the struggle for verbal control between a champion talker and a brilliant recorder of talk, he calls attention to moral issues at gossip's heart. I have suggested before gossip's function as resource of the subordinated. Those to whom society allows no power retain the possibility of talking—perhaps only in whispers, behind closed doors—about people who run things. Always feeling Johnson his superior, characteristically subordinating his immediate desires to his mentor's, Boswell reasserts himself by collecting and setting down stories: an activity comparable to gossip.

The concept of "meaning" in a human life implies meaning *to* someone. Gossipers generate meanings, which they may choose to keep within their group. Boswell encourages his readers to share the long process of reconciling his perception of Johnson's moral and intellectual grandeur with his own assertion not only of autonomy but of mastery. Showing himself as manipulator of social encounters (the famous meeting with Wilkes, for example) and of conversation ("If, Sir, you were shut up in a castle, and a newborn child with you, what would you do?"), but most of all as controller of significance, Boswell raises questions about what personal narrative means to the narrator and to the subject of narration. His self-exposure becomes his authority. The impossibility of his disappearing from the text demonstrates his presence at the narrative's center: the interpretive consciousness declares itself integral to the story's import. At the narrative's heart lies Boswell's discovery of his own power in an asymmetrical relationship with an overwhelmingly powerful man. Here too, public and private intersect. The biographer shows what precedes the public act of writing. One can play the fool, he demonstrates, without being one. His consistent self-subordination in day-to-day intercourse with Johnson allows him the verbal mastery of his book: a pattern paralleling the contrast he shows in Johnson, whose private inadequacies make his public performance more astounding. The art and the communicated knowledge of *The Life of Samuel Johnson, LL.D.* involve the interplay of two lives as well as the twining of public and private in each of them.

The matters I have been discussing—the narrator's relation to text and audience, the nature of meaning in story, the use of story as mastery—belong to fiction as well as to biography and gossip. Boswell's mode, obviously, does not dominate all biographies. But the problems to which it calls attention, of the narrator's connection with subject, audience, and text, resurface in biographies quite unlike *The Life of Samuel Johnson, LL.D.*

Such as, for example, W. Jackson Bate's late twentieth-century *Samuel Johnson*, a magisterial work which, like Boswell's, assesses the man and his achievement, but emerges with rather different conclusions and employs utterly different techniques. Some of the differences derive from greater distance in time, lack of personal knowledge—some, but not all. In Boswell's biography, the process of interpretation that preoccupies the narrator comes to absorb the reader. Bate provides consistent conclusions rather than a view of the process leading to them. His interpretation appears to have preceded the writing of the biography; Boswell, who starts with an attitude of "worship" toward his great subject, only gradually works out the meaning of his text—a meaning which obviously includes himself. Bate rarely uses the first-person-singular pronoun. He prefers the plural: a "we" invoking the community of cultivated readers, implicitly claiming for Johnson that universality which Boswell too assumed. Bate's Johnson takes on moral and intellectual stature comparable to Boswell's, but Bate emphasizes pain, privation, and struggle: the inner life of suffering rather than the public life of triumph. He claims complete continuity between "public" and "private." And, unlike Boswell, he never deviates from a confident, authoritative tone—although one informed with passion.

Psychic life, in the twentieth century, provides almost as rich material for speculation as sex life. That elegant form of gossip called psychoanalysis, in which a patient supplies a fertile flow of intimate data and the analyst collaborates in constructing a story from it, has deeply influenced twentieth-century imaginations. Bate in his biography eschews vulgar psychoanalytic speculation, calling attention to the ease with which minds informed by Freud leap to sexual explanations for psychological peculiarities, and providing more careful hypotheses himself. Yet he invites and helps the reader to see even in trivial episodes of Johnson's life evidence of a painfully divided man.

In an essay entitled "Literary Criticism and Methodology," the linguist Thomas Pavel, trying to distinguish between two kinds of literary criticism ("optimistic," which assumes the possibility of saying something about a text, and "apprehensive," operating with opposed assumptions), compares "optimistic" criticism with gossip. He means nothing pejorative: "one can recognize," he points out, "that there is such a thing as 'good' gossip; gossip that correctly applies the rules of the game." "Good" gossip demands that the speaker "stay within the limits of the subject matter and . . . tell the truth"; also "that gossip-hypotheses be as specific as possible and that the evidence for them be a matter of common knowledge. . . . Thus gossip (good gossip) is an informal exercise in hypothesis devising and evidence finding. . . . Its purpose is the understanding of the person or the situation discussed." "Basic gossip" reports facts and constructs simple hypotheses about them; "sophisticated gossip" involves "the devising of elaborate, unexpected hypotheses, often supported only by tenuous evidence." In the equivalent kind of literary criticism, "purpose is not purely cognitive. The reader does not expect to learn only true facts and correct explanations about the literary work, but, more important, to be put in the literary mood, to appreciate the atmosphere of a specific work or, even more generally, of a given literary group or period. One expects this type of criticism to familiarise its reader with the prevalent literary climate in the same way that gossip adjusts people to the surrounding social climate."

Much more than Boswell, Bate (who admires Boswell, but implies his own greater interpretive power) appears to consider biography and criticism intimately related activities. Pavel's comments about criticism apply precisely to the biographical technique of *Samuel Johnson*, which assumes the possibility of saying something illuminating about an actual person. The book's hypotheses rest often on ambiguous evidence, yet they persuasively elucidate Johnson's nature and context. For example:

> In January (1740) Johnson was back at Lichfield, again visiting Walmesley and seeing Molly Aston. But even if he continued to

delay returning to London, something had to be done about money. Lacking any other alternative, he and his mother made arrangements to mortgage the house. . . . There is no indication that Sarah herself needed to do this. Living very cheaply, she seemed able to survive on the small income that the bookshop still brought her. The mortgage was certainly made at Johnson's own urging, and the request could hardly increase his self-respect. He was now thirty-one. He had earned nothing for over half a year. Owing to his own indolence, he and—because of him— Sarah were now capitalizing on the sole asset that remained to them.

Neither Hawkins nor Boswell mentions this episode. Bate, interpreting the bare fact of a mortgage on the Lichfield house, makes much from little. His vocabulary hints tentativeness: "There is no indication," "seemed," "certainly" (implying considerable uncertainty), "hardly." His general hypothesis of Johnson's mental distress at this period subsumes the financial transaction, which then becomes further evidence for it.

I do not mean to quarrel with the interpretation or with its method: Bate's capacity to make the most of small detail creates his book's richness, and his reading of events, like his reading of texts, sounds unfailingly plausible although rarely indisputable. Lives, like texts, demand rereading as time passes; what Bate sees in Johnson's career epitomizes twentieth-century vision. My point is simply that this kind of interpretation, like that of the criticism Pavel cites, belongs to the repertoire of gossip.

The point becomes clearer in relation to the kind of biographical material traditionally associated with gossip: for instance, the matter of Johnson's marriage. Hawkins hints that he married for money, suggesting that Elizabeth Porter's first husband "left her, if not well jointured, so provided for, as made a match with her to a man in Johnson's circumstances desirable"; he says that "little can now be remembered" of her "personal charms," but that since Johnson probably didn't see well enough to notice, any deficiency of beauty would hardly have mattered to him. Boswell describes Mrs. Porter (inaccurately) as "double the age of Johnson," adding that since "her person and manner, as described to me by the late Mr. Garrick, were by no means pleasing to others, she must have had a superiority of understanding and talents, as she certainly inspired him with a more than ordinary passion." The marriage, Boswell says, "was a very imprudent scheme, both on account of their disparity of years, and her want of fortune. Four pages later, he quotes Garrick's grotesque description.

Both these accounts (like all biographies before Bate's) evade the erotic, with Hawkins hinting prudential motivation and Boswell hypothesizing intellectual appeal ("superiority of understanding and talents") as the most plausible explanation for Johnson's "passion." Bate confronts the issue more directly. He notes Mrs. Thrale's testimony about Johnson's extraordinary awareness of female appearance and dress: however bad his eyes, Johnson could see his wife. He adduces evidence from another observer (William Shaw, a clergyman whom Johnson helped and who subsequently wrote a memoir of the great man) that at the time of the marriage Tetty "was still young and handsome." And he offers his own explanation, beginning with a general demonstration of Johnson's unusual capacity for gratitude and moving to the particular. "Certainly gratitude was for Johnson a powerful element in this marriage of seventeen years, which was the first of the three or four things (the next was the new career he was to start in London, largely because of the responsibility he felt for Tetty) that really pulled him out and saved him from the self-destructive state into which he had been sunk for so long. From the start, . . . Elizabeth Jervis Porter had given him help and confidence." In other words, Bate accounts for an emotional fact in emotional terms: a kind of feeling we know Johnson to have demonstrated in other situations may explain the intense feeling he attached to his wife.

Again, the hypothesis rests on little direct evidence. Bate recalls Boswell's report that Mrs. Porter valued Johnson's conversation, declaring him the most sensible man she ever saw, and ignored his grotesque appearance: thus, presumably, she gave him confidence. Johnson worked as a tutor for two months before his marriage and reclaimed the books he had left at Oxford five and a half years before: slender proof that "things had made a turn for the better" as a result of Elizabeth Porter's faith in him. Like Bate's interpretation of the mortgage episode, his understanding of Johnson's marriage derives from his vision of the sage as a man in recurrent (almost chronic) psychic crisis, ever needing to be "pulled . . . out." Mrs. Porter's apparent capacity to relieve that crisis becomes, therefore, the ground of Johnson's feeling for her.

From a twentieth-century point of view, Bate's explanation sounds more plausible than Hawkins' and more convincing than Boswell's. But all three accounts conform to the model of Pavel's "sophisticated gossip" and appeal to the reader's interest not only in facts of human experience but in meanings attributable to these facts. Bate's capacity to provide a single, complex, coherent interpretation for Johnson's human diversity energizes his biography. It also answers one of the same human needs as gossip.

Bate understands Johnson's life as a "parable"—that is to say, he *makes* it a parable—and Johnson's writing as continuous with his life. "Hence in the moral writings—as in all of his greater writing or as in the parable of his life generally—we always sense two fundamental values, not because they are preached but because they are coming to us with the force of example. One is the potential freedom of man. . . . The second value, sustaining and rendering practical the first, is expressed in the simplest and finest of his maxims: 'The first step in greatness is to be honest.'" To write a critical biography implies not only specific belief in the connection between the individual subject and his or her work but general faith in the intimate connection of life and art. Boswell assumes that the greatness of Johnson's moral writings testifies to the grandeur of his moral being; Bate uses the complexity of Johnson's moral experience to discover the intricacy of his published prose. Although he does not reduce the mass of published writings to a single model, he finds everywhere supporting evidence for his sense of Johnson's struggle against his own "self demand," his unceasing effort to keep himself psychically afloat. One example, in the *Preface to Shakespeare*: "Here we have continuing for pages what before we found more often in particular sentences or paragraphs: a grasping, against strong internal pressures, for certitude, control, balance, and order. We sense the whole body being involved, as though he were trying to pull himself above the surface. Hence the tamped-down finality as he phrases convictions based on a lifetime of experience." Taken out of context, these observations, except for such specific references as "pages," might as plausibly concern the "parable" of Johnson's life as the nature of his work. The work itself now dramatizes the process of being "pulled out" that the life reiterates. The interpretive act involved in Bate's criticism duplicates that of the purely biographical portions of his book. Both draw from assumptions about discourse which also govern gossip. Both, like gossip, try to win assent by assuming it ("We sense . . .").

Bate includes stories which Boswell omits: for example, the vignette about Johnson's imitating a kangaroo on the journey through the Hebrides. He provides a chapter on "Wit and Humor," emphasizing Johnson's comic gifts. The Johnson he presents does not spend every minute in melancholy, though Bate insists on the melancholy strain underlying all else. But this biography earns its epigraph (from Pythagoras): "What is your warrant for valuing any part of my experience and rejecting the rest? . . . If I had done so, you would never have heard my name." Bate shows Johnson as one who valued his own experience in its entirety, taking everything seriously (comedy, of course, being one mode of taking things seriously), and he shows himself as likewise valuing the entire experience of his complicated, awe-inspiring subject. The biography thus implies for its readers the desirability of understanding, valuing, interpreting their own lives.

All good biography illumines every reader's life by generating intimate awareness of another. Bate's insistent "we" encourages intimacy, suggesting his own identification, allowing the reader's, with his subject. His emphasis on the necessary difficulties of middle age and on the problem of loneliness, particularly that of increasing age, calls attention to the universality of dilemmas he understands Johnson to have faced. If Boswell generates complexity and power by separating himself from his subject, insisting on his role as witness and recorder, reminding his readers of the mastery implicit in acts of interpretation, Bate achieves his effects by virtually opposite means. In conviction and attitude, he finally almost merges with his subject. His empathetic grasp of Johnson's suffering and triumph invites readers too to see themselves in Johnson, Johnson in themselves. By accretion of small detail and by contemplative dwelling on detail (Johnson's mother took a mortgage on her house . . .), Bate constructs a myth of heroism different from Boswell's. Boswell reveals the discrepancy of private fallibility and public achievement. Bate insists that private and public, life and work, participate in a single meaning. His vision of heroism represents not an alternative to fallibility but a mode of life both containing and transcending fallibility; he makes of that vision an aesthetic construct and a moral statement. Affirming shared humanity and demonstrating that sharing by examination and interpretation of detail, Bate embodies in yet another way the positive values of gossip, as a process of interpretation and as a humanizing activity.

Why do commentators value written forms of observational narrative but at best only joke about gossip which shares such narrative's values? Dr. Johnson, in his familiar exposition of biography's importance, insists on the significance of trivial detail and on the imaginative power of specific knowledge about other people. In a less well-known *Rambler*, on the other hand, he deplores narrative about others as an element of conversation. People enjoy it, he admits; but they shouldn't.

> He who has stored his memory with slight anecdotes, private incidents, and personal particularities, seldom fails to find his audience favorable. Almost every man listens with eagerness to contemporary history; for almost every man has some real or imaginary connection with a celebrated character, some desire to advance, or oppose a rising name. Vanity often cooperates with curiosity. He that is a hearer in one place qualifies himself to

become a speaker in another; for though he cannot comprehend a series of argument, or transport the volatile spirit of wit without evaporation, he yet thinks himself able to treasure up the various incidents of a story, and pleases his hopes with the information which he shall give to some inferior society.

Narratives are for the most part heard without envy, because they are not supposed to imply any intellectual qualities above the common rate. To be acquainted with facts not yet echoed by plebeian mouths, may happen to one man as well as to another, and to relate them when they are known, has in appearance so little difficulty, that every one concludes himself equal to the task.

Narrative in speech requires no intellectual gifts; moreover, Johnson goes on to imply, it tends to reduce its subjects to the same level as its hearers, encouraging the pernicious myth of equality.

The *Rambler* essay on biography argues that small facts provide the biographer's best material, since they compose the texture of human life. Johnson emphasizes how much we all share as human beings; biography, he believes, should stress this truth. In the biographical text, he finds such concern not reductive but instructive. Nothing is too little for so little a creature as man, he told Boswell. Yet the talker who reports man's littleness out loud wins only his reproach.

The biography essay insists that a "judicious and faithful narrative" of *any* human life would be useful. A few months earlier, however, Johnson had argued that writers of novels—a genre based, in his view, on imitation rather than invention—must take care choosing specific lives to delineate because of their writings' imaginative potency. "If the power of example is so great as to take possession of the memory by a kind of violence, and produce effects almost without the intervention of the will, care ought to be taken that when the choice is unrestrained, the best examples only should be exhibited; and that which is likely to operate should not be mischievous or uncertain in its effects." Why should novels prove so much more dangerous than biographies? Perhaps because they involve the imagination more intensely; their readers, Johnson tells us, include "the young, the ignorant, and the idle," all susceptible to the lures of fancy. He does not tell us who reads biography.

Let me recapitulate this series of observations. Stories about other people reported in speech attract ready audiences because everyone feels some connection to well-known people, because the hearers can anticipate their own subsequent roles as narrators of the same stories, and because those hearers feel no envy of the narrator's gifts: he needs no gifts, they believe, and Johnson appears to share their conviction. Such tales falsify experience by simplifying it and by suggesting that those talked about have the same flaws as those talking. Stories about other people presented in the guise of printed fiction attract the gullible; the novelist therefore must take responsibility for making characters and actions in fiction instructive, for presenting positive models of conduct. Stories about other people in biography cannot be too trivial; they illustrate the ways in which small actions define character and comprise experience.

The implicit differentiations here involve both author and audience, different kinds of authority, different kinds of receptivity. Johnson appears to imagine oral narrative as communicated in coffee houses: a limited public setting. Novels reach a larger, more indiscriminate public; biography appeals to a group which Johnson fails to define but which he apparently trusts. The transmitters of narrative take their places in a posited hierarchy of authority, a hierarchy which illuminates the subjects of women and of gossip.

The biographer's authority exceeds the novelist's because of the weight of didactic tradition accruing to his genre (I use the masculine pronoun because Johnson entirely assumes it) and because he grounds his narrative in fact. Johnson takes for granted both the didactic intent and the didactic effect of a life story in writing. The biographer imposes pattern on experience to declare the comprehensibility of human existence. Learning of other people, we learn of ourselves. Lacking a long formal tradition to authorize his enterprise, the novelist, with more dubious purpose than the biographer, risks contamination by association with the morally suspect mode of romance: as Johnson reproachfully observes, novels too often make love the spring of action. And novelists rely, of course, on the dangerous power of imagination: to put it bluntly, they *lie*.

Both novelist and biographer, however, by assuming the responsibility and the power of the written word, exceed in authority the conversational narrator for whom Johnson expresses patronizing contempt. Johnson imagines this narrator too as male; he does not even bother to discuss those jabbering females evoked by his dictionary's striking definition of *gossip*, which I quoted earlier ("One who runs about tattling like women at a lying-in"). Such women, in Johnson's representative view, would lack all semblance of authority. Conversing only with one another, they confine themselves to a more private sphere than that of the male story-teller who circulates in coffee houses to relate the foibles of public men, existing therefore at least on the fringes of the public life that tests human worth—*male* worth. Women share secrets, hiding from scrutiny. And—Johnson doesn't say this, but many others do—they deal in scandal, thus raising questions of motive and the possibility of fanciful exaggeration. Critics implicitly grant the biographer moral motivation; they allow its possibility for the novelist, despite suspicion that the fiction-writer may stress pleasure more than instruction. The coffee-house story-teller, Johnson suggests, wishes to make himself important and to reduce the stature of those greater than he. But in the eyes of their critics, female gossips, their specific utterances only hypothesized, conceal destructive purposes, existing thus at the bottom of the moral hierarchy as well as of the closely connected hierarchy of authority.

Public writing on the whole enjoyed higher status than did private talk. Eliza Haywood, writing early in the century specifically about gossip, suggests a possible justification for the oral mode by raising the question, "Will the Knowledge of what other People do make us wiser or happier?"— only to answer it, without further explanation, by insisting that abundant examples, both positive and negative, exist already in writing. Examples in writing of course possess the stability necessarily lacking in oral utterance; their implications can be more sternly controlled. Women's gossip seems dangerous not only because it belongs to women but because it belongs to the unpredictable realm of talk, talk made more unpredictable by taking place in domestic rather than public settings. When Addison speaks of "female oratory," his irony focuses on just this aspect of women's conversation: he considers such talk negligible precisely because it is *not* oratory, not public performance.

Explicitly, the body of moral doctrine I have been citing draws on an acknowledged standard of social decorum to sanction disapproval of gossip. The implications of the doctrine, however, go far beyond propriety. To summarize: the eighteenth-century attack on gossip suggests the superiority of the verbal mode epitomized by those who can read Latin and consider public matters; it hints the inadequacy of female understanding as well as of female talk; it declares the reprehensible nature of concern with human detail if such concern issues in speech; it preaches a doctrine of repression in the service of communal welfare, in the interests of that "society" generally assumed to define value. If the moralizers leave a few loose ends in such comments as Steele's connection of authorship with curiosity and Fordyce's recognition of female insight, they yet display a striking unanimity in their distaste for gossip and in the grounds of that distaste.

Women can write as well as talk, of course, although Dr. Johnson barely acknowledged the fact; and they wrote novels beginning early in the eighteenth century, sometimes anonymously or under pseudonyms, but sometimes attaching their own names. Curiosity; avid interest in other people, their lives, the small manifestations of their personalities; close observation and nice discrimination—the qualities alleged to account for the nature of women's conversation now fueled their writing (as well as that of their male contemporaries) and apparently interested readers male and female, old and young. Even the malice supposed to underlie gossip could provide energy for the novel. In deeper ways than Dr. Johnson may consciously have realized, the novel embodied troubling possibilities.

Chronology

1709	Samuel Johnson born September 7 in Lichfield, Staffordshire.
1717	Enters Lichfield Grammar School.
1728–29	Attends Pembroke College, Oxford, but does not take a degree.
1733	Translates Lobo's *Voyage to Abyssinia*.
1735	Marries Elizabeth Jervis Porter, a widow.
1736	Opens a school at Edial, and begins *Irene*.
1737	Moves to London, along with David Garrick; his wife joins him soon after.
1738	Begins writing for *Gentleman's Magazine*, and publishes "London."
1739–43	Earns living writing miscellaneous journalistic pieces, some of which are biographical sketches.
1740	James Boswell born October 29 in Edinburgh.
1744	Johnson publishes *The Life of Mr. Richard Savage*.
1745	Johnson submits proposals for an edition of Shakespeare.
1746	Johnson signs a contract for the *Dictionary*.
1749	Johnson publishes "The Vanity of Human Wishes." His *Irene* is produced by Garrick.
1750–52	Johnson founds, and does most of the writing for, *The Rambler*, a periodical.

1752	Johnson's wife dies, leaving him to care for her blind friend, Anna Williams.
1753–58	Boswell attends the University of Edinburgh.
1755	Johnson receives an honorary degree from Oxford, and publishes the *Dictionary*.
1756	Johnson makes further proposals for an edition of Shakespeare.
1758–59	Boswell studies law at the University of Edinburgh.
1758–60	Johnson contributes the *Idler* series of essays to the *Universal Chronicle*, a weekly periodical.
1759	Johnson's mother dies; he publishes *Rasselas*. Boswell studies civil law at the University of Glasgow.
1760	Boswell makes his first visit to London, and converts for a short time to Roman Catholicism.
1762	The King awards Johnson a yearly pension of £ 300.
1763	Boswell meets Johnson in a bookstore. Boswell collaborates with Andrew Erskine in publishing *Letters Between The Honourable Andrew Erskine and James Boswell, Esq*. He goes to Utrecht to study civil law.
1764	Johnson and Sir Joshua Reynolds found The (Literary) Club. Boswell goes on a Grand Tour of Germany and Switzerland, and meets Voltaire and Rousseau.
1765	Johnson publishes his edition of Shakespeare. He meets the Thrales.
1765–66	Boswell continues Grand Tour, and meets Pasquale Paoli in Corsica. He returns from Continent, is admitted to the Scottish bar, and begins practice in Edinburgh.
1768	Boswell publishes *An Account of Corsica*.
1769	Boswell marries Margaret Montgomerie.
1773	Boswell's daughter Veronica born; he is elected to The Club. Boswell and Johnson tour the Highlands and the Hebrides.

1774	Johnson publishes *The Patriot*, and tours Wales with the Thrales. Boswell's daughter Euphemia born.
1775	Johnson publishes *Journey to the Western Islands of Scotland*. Boswell's son Alexander born.
1776	Boswell's son David born.
1777	Johnson begins work on *The Lives of the Poets*.
1777–83	Boswell contributes a series of essays, *The Hypochondriack* to *The London Magazine*, a periodical.
1778	Boswell's son James born.
1779	Johnson publishes the first four volumes of *The Lives of the Poets*.
1781	Johnson publishes the final six volumes of *The Lives of the Poets*.
1782	Boswell's father dies and he succeeds as Laird of Auchinleck.
1783	Johnson has a stroke, from which he recovers.
1784	Johnson dies on December 13, and is buried in Westminster Abbey.
1785	Boswell publishes *Journal of a Tour to the Hebrides*.
1786	Boswell moves to London, where he is admitted to the English bar.
1788	Boswell is appointed Recorder of Carlisle.
1789	Boswell's wife dies.
1791	Boswell publishes *The Life of Samuel Johnson, LL.D.*
1795	Boswell dies in London on May 19.

Contributors

HAROLD BLOOM, Sterling Professor of the Humanities at Yale University, is the author of *The Anxiety of Influence, Poetry and Repression*, and many other volumes of literary criticism. His forthcoming study, *Freud: Transference and Authority*, attempts a fullscale reading of all of Freud's major writings. A MacArthur Prize Fellow, he is the general editor of *The Chelsea House Library of Literary Criticism*.

RALPH W. RADER is professor of English at the University of California at Berkeley and the author of *Tennyson's Maud: The Biographical Genesis*.

PAUL K. ALKON is Leo S. Bing Professor of English at the University of Southern California. He is the author of *Defoe and Fictional Time*.

FREDERICK A. POTTLE has been Sterling Professor Emeritus of English at Yale University since 1966 and is coeditor of the Yale editions of the Private Papers of James Boswell. He is also the author of *Pride and Negligence: The History of the Boswell Papers* and *The Idiom of Poetry*.

RICHARD B. SCHWARTZ is Professor of English at the University of Wisconsin, Madison. His books include *Samuel Johnson and the New Science* and *Samuel Johnson and the Problem of Evil*.

WILLIAM R. SIEBENSCHUH is Associate Professor of English at Case Western Reserve University, Cleveland, Ohio, and the author of *Form and Purpose in Boswell's Biographical Works*.

FRANK BRADY is Professor of English at the Graduate Center of the City University of New York and the chairman of the Editorial Committee and coeditor of the Yale editions of the Private Papers of James Boswell. His books include *Boswell's Political Career* and *James Boswell: The Later Years*.

PATRICIA MEYER SPACKS is Professor of English and department head at Yale University. Her books include *The Female Imagination* and *Gossip*.

Bibliography

Alkon, Paul K. "Boswellian Time." *Studies in Burke and His Time* 14 (1973): 239–56.

Altick, Richard D. *Lives and Letters: A History of Literary Biography in England and America.* New York: Alfred A. Knopf, 1965.

Bate, W. Jackson. *Samuel Johnson.* New York: Harcourt Brace Jovanovich, 1975.

Bell, Robert H. "Boswell's Notes Toward a Supreme Fiction from *London Journal* to *Life of Johnson*." *Modern Language Quarterly* 38 (1977): 132–48.

Brack, O. M., Jr. and Robert E. Kelley, eds. *The Early Biographies of Samuel Johnson,* Iowa City: University of Iowa Press, 1974.

Brady, Frank. "Boswell's Self-Presentation and His Critics." *Studies in English Literature* 12 (1972): 545–55.

Brooks, A. Russell. *James Boswell.* New York: Twayne, 1971.

Butt, John. *Biography in the Hands of Walton, Johnson, and Boswell.* Ewing Lectures. Los Angeles: University of California Press, 1966.

Clifford, James L., ed. *Biography as an Art: Selected Criticism, 1560–1960.* New York: Oxford University Press, 1962.

————. *Young Sam Johnson.* New York: McGraw-Hill, 1955.

Damrosch, Leopold, Jr. "The Life of Johnson: An Anti-Theory." *Eighteenth-Century Studies* 6 (1973):486-505.

Dowling, William C. *The Boswellian Hero.* Athens: University of Georgia Press, 1979.

————. *Language and Logos in Boswell's "Life of Johnson."* Princeton: Princeton University Press, 1981.

Evans, Bergen B. "Dr. Johnson's Theory of Biography." *Review of English Studies* 10 (1934): 301–310.

Fussell, Paul, Jr. "The Force of Literary Memory in Boswell's *London Journal*." *Studies in English Literature* 2 (1962): 351–57.

Greene, Donald J. "Reflections on a Literary Anniversary." *Queens Quarterly* 70 (1963): 198–208.

Hart, Francis R. "Boswell and the Romantics: A Chapter in the History of Biographical Theory." *English Literary History* 27 (1960): 44–65.

Krutch, Joseph Wood. "On the Talk of Samuel Johnson and His Friends." *American Scholar* 13 (1944): 263-72.

Lipking, Lawrence. 1975. "Art, Morals, Madness: Some Problems in Writing the Lives of Pope, Johnson, and Blake." Paper presented at Modern Language Association Convention.

Mallory, George. *Boswell the Biographer*. London: Smith, Elder and Co., 1912.

Olney, James. *Metaphors of the Self: The Meaning of Autobiography*. Princeton: Princeton University Press, 1972.

Passler, David L. *Time, Form and Style in Boswell's "Life of Johnson."* New Haven: Yale University Press, 1971.

Pottle, Frederick A. "The Power of Memory in Boswell and Scott." In *Essays on the Eighteenth Century Presented to David Nichol Smith in Honour of His Seventieth Birthday*. Oxford: Clarendon Press, 1945.

Reid, Benjamin L. "Johnson's Life of Boswell." *Kenyon Review* 18 (1956): 546–75.

Siebenschuh, William R. *Form and Purpose in Boswell's Biographical Works*. Berkeley and Los Angeles: University of California Press, 1972.

Stauffer, Donald A. *The Art of Biography in Eighteenth Century England*. 2 vols. Princeton: Princeton University Press, 1941.

Tracy, Clarence. "Boswell: The Cautious Empiricist." In *The Triumph of Culture: 18th-Century Perspectives*, edited by Paul Fritz and David Williams. Toronto: Hakkert, 1972.

Waingrow, Marshall, ed. *The Correspondence and Other Papers of James Boswell Relating to the Making of the "Life of Johnson."* New York: McGraw-Hill, 1969.

Wimsatt, W. K. "Images of Samuel Johnson." *English Literary History* 41 (1974): 359-74.

———. "The Fact Imagined: James Boswell." In *Hateful Contraries: Studies in Literature and Criticism*. Lexington: University of Kentucky Press, 1965.

Acknowledgments

"Literary Form in Factual Narrative: The Example of Boswell's *Johnson*" by Ralph W. Rader. from *Essays in Eighteenth-Century Biography*, edited by Philip B. Daghlian, copyright © 1968 by Indiana University Press. Reprinted by permission.

"Boswell's Control of Aesthetic Distance" by Paul K. Alkon from *University of Toronto Quarterly* 38, no. 2 (January 1969), copyright © 1969 by University of Toronto Press. Reprinted by permission of the author and the University of Toronto Press.

"The *Life of Johnson:* Art and Authenticity" by Frederick A. Pottle from *Twentieth Century Interpretations of Boswell's "Life of Johnson,"* edited by James L. Clifford, copyright © 1970 by Prentice-Hall, Inc. Reprinted by permission of the author.

"Johnson's Johnson" by Richard B. Schwartz from *Boswell's Johnson: A Preface to the "Life"* by Richard B. Schwartz, copyright © 1978 by Board of Regents of the University of Wisconsin System. Reprinted by permission of University of Wisconsin Press.

"Factual Appearances and Fictional Effects: Boswell's *Life of Johnson*" by William R. Siebenschuh from *Fictional Techniques anf Factual Works* by William R. Siebenschuh, copyright © 1983 by the University of Georgia Press. Reprinted by permission of The University of Chicago Press.

"James Boswell: Theory and Practice of Biography" (originally entitled "The Life") by Frank Brady from *James Boswell: The Later Years, 1769-1795,* copyright © 1984 by Frank Brady, Reprinted by permission.

"Gossip; (originally entitled "Biography: Moral and Physical Truth") by Patricia Meyer Spacks from *Gossip,* copyright © 1985 by Patricia Meyer Spacks. Reprinted by permission of Alfred A. Knopf.

155

Index

Abrams, Meyer Howard, 73
Addison, Joseph, 16, 70, 95, 132, 145
Aeneid (Virgil), 79
Aesthetic distance, Boswell's control of,
    vii, 35–51; from Boswell as narrator,
    43–51, 84, 115; from Johnson, 35–46,
    51; and intellectual, moral, and emo-
    tional distance, 40–51; and temporal
    distance, 39–40, 44–45
Anderson, Robert, 121
Anecdotes of Johnson (Piozzi), 2, 63–64, 65,
    99, 111, 140; and anecdote, 26, 99; on
    Boswell, 2; Boswell on, 48, 94, 120,
    122, 129; compared to *Life,* 13–14,
    15, 19, 26, 27, 108, 123–24; presenta-
    tion of Johnson, 13–14, 19, 26, 27,
    99, 108
Aristotle, 10, 18, 21, 129
Augustine, 73, 99
Bate, Walter Jackson, 127–28, 130,
    137–42; *Samuel Johnson,* 137–42
Beggar's Opera (Gay), 41–42, 132–33; Cap-
    tain Macheath, 50, 133
Biography, and aesthetic distance, 27,
    35, 36, 126–27, 142; anecdotal, 98–99,
    101–2, 134; art, morality, and knowl-
    edge in, 128–29; and autobiography,
    35, 61–63, 78; and character, 11, 16,
    21, 28–30, 37, 93, 126, 128, 142; criti-
    cal, 99–102, 141; and drama, 10, 98;
    and epic, 10; ethical, 98–102, 125,
    128, 131–32, 144; and factual narra-
    tive, 9–10, 31–34, 97–98, 125, 128;
    and fiction, vii, 31–32, 95, 97–98,
    125, 126, 128, 137, 144, 145; and
    hero, 21, 35, 78, 79, 85, 86, 89,
    100–101, 111, 112, 113, 118, 130–31,
    134, 142; and memory, 62–63, 98;
    and narrator, 105, 123, 126–28, 133,
    134, 142, 144; and novel, 10, 98, 125,
    126, 128, 143–46; and pleasure, 9,

18–32, 126; and psychology, 99, 128,
    137–42; relation of, to history, litera-
    ture, and "truth," vii, viii, 6, 7,
    9–11, 28–34, 74, 78–80, 85, 95, 98,
    100, 105, 118, 122, 125–28, 134;
    "total," 7; as universal, 10, 11,
    28–34, 74, 137, 142. *See also* Aesthetic
    distance; Gossip
Blair, Hugh, 115
Blake, William, 74, 76, 100
Boerhaave, Herman, 64
Booth, Wayne, 37
Boswell, James, attitude of, toward John-
    son, 4, 7, 11, 12, 27, 46, 53, 109, 111,
    131; and biography, 7, 16, 53,
    97–102; character of, 4, 53–54, 115,
    117; as a character, 46–50, 84, 85,
    113, 115–16, 131, 135; first meeting
    of, with Johnson, 17, 80–84; and Lon-
    don, 23, 42, 48, 49, 50, 54, 117; mem-
    ory of, 13, 55–59, 133; and "na-
    ïveté," 115, 135; parting of, with
    Johnson, at Harwich, 31, 88; and re-
    ligion, 48–49, 74, 91, 120, 128; self-
    consciousness of, vii, 1, 36, 116;
    static view of personality, 62, 107;
    style of, 6–7, 41, 114–16; as a writer,
    54, 113–18. *Works*: journals and
    notes, 41, 53–59, 63, 79–85, 90–92,
    99, 101, 102–5, 123, 124; "Memoirs
    of James Boswell," 118; "Memoirs
    of Pascal Paoli," 101, 102, 116. *See
    also* Aesthetic distance; Biography;
    Journal; Life; London Journal
Boswell, John, 102
Brady, Frank, vii–viii, 126
Bronson, Bertrand, 64
Burke, Edmund, 98, 110, 113, 122
Burney, Charles, 119
Burney, Fanny, 26, 27
Capote, Truman, 33, 34